THE CENTERS OF CIVILIZATION SERIES

Florence

IN THE AGE OF DANTE

IN THE AGE OF

DANTE

by Paul G. Ruggiers

NORMAN

UNIVERSITY OF OKLAHOMA PRESS

BY PAUL G. RUGGIERS

Michele Barbi, *Life of Dante* (translator) (Berkeley, 1954)
Modern American Reader (editor, with Irving Ribner) (New York, 1959)
Florence in the Age of Dante (Norman, 1964)

Library of Congress Catalog Card Number: 64–20761

For Carol Daube Sutton

Foreword

I CANNOT BELIEVE that my Antonio Loschi, who has seen Florence, or anyone else who has seen it, can deny that it is the flower, the most beautiful part, of Italy—unless he is utterly mad. What city, not merely in Italy, but in all the world, is more securely placed within its circle of walls, more proud in its *palazzi*, more bedecked with churches, more beautiful in its architecture, more imposing in its gates, richer in piazzas, happier in its wide streets, greater in its people, more glorious in its citizenry, more inexhaustible in wealth, more fertile in its fields? . . . What city has been more active in professions, more admirable, generally, in all things? What city without a seaport ships out so much goods? Where is business a greater enterprise, or richer in variety of stuffs, or carried on with more astuteness and sagacity? Where are men more illustrious? And—let me not be tiresome—more distinguished in affairs, valiant in arms, strong in just rule, and renowned? Where can you find a Dante, a Petrarch, a Boccaccio? Tell me, I beg you, oh infamous monster, to what place, to what men can you assign the highest place of honor in Italy, if you say that Florence is the off-scouring of Italy? Would to God that, if Florence's liberty and power remain at their present glory, the rest of Italy could so improve that the Florentines, by comparing themselves with it, would see themselves as

ix

the dregs of Italy. But since in this corruptible world such grandeur is utterly impossible, be ashamed, thou foulest of foul men, for calling the Florentines the lees of Italy, when in fact they are its one and only glory.

Coluccio Salutati
From *Invective against Antonio Loschi of Vicenze* (1400)

Acknowledgments

I AM GRATEFUL for the liberal terms of a Fulbright Fellowship (1961–62) which provided me with the freedom and the leisure to write this book. I have a special debt of gratitude to Professor Ulrich Middeldorf, director of the German Institute of Art History in Florence, who generously made the facilities of his library available to me, and to Miss Cipriana Scelba, directress of the American Commission for Cultural Exchange in Rome, whose organization opened many doors for me.

PAUL G. RUGGIERS

Norman, Oklahoma
March 1, 1964

xi

Contents

Florence

IN THE AGE OF DANTE

1. The Matrix of History

IN THE YEAR 1212, after the excommunication of Emperor Otto IV, Pope Innocent III advanced the name of Frederick of Hohenstaufen, king of Sicily, as the new head of the empire. Those who were loyal to Otto took a name based upon that of his family and called themselves Guelfs, while those who accepted Frederick named themselves Ghibellines after a place long associated with the Hohenstaufen line.

In Italy the party names took on meanings dictated by varying political exigencies. The term "Ghibelline" continued to signify the imperialist alignment. "Guelf," however, lost its association with the dynastic German quarrel and came to designate supporters of the papacy in its struggle with the empire.

Crystallized more or less along these lines throughout the peninsula, the division into parties within Florence assumed its own focus in the problem of civic autonomy, a goal towards which the city had been moving in the previous century. In general, the higher nobility, adherent to the emperor and seeking his assistance, made up the Ghibelline party; the minor nobility and the rising merchant class, anxious to be free of the burden of empire and therefore supporters of the papacy, comprised the Guelf party. Since Florence was in its historical development democratic in spirit and instinct, the story of the commune at the outset

3

of our period traces out the gradual submission of the old imperial nobility to the goals of its powerful merchant citizenry.

The precipitating factor and, according to Dante, the cause of the split into two parties in his city was the quarrel between the Amidei and the Buondelmonti. To settle rancor between the two families, a marriage had been arranged in the customary manner between the young people of the two clans. The young man, regretting the betrothal and tempted to another love, dared to renounce his pledge. On the day arranged for his marriage, scorning the kinsmen of the girl to whom he had been betrothed, he delivered a ring to his new lady, violating his old contract and originating a new one. His death was decided from the moment when Mosca de' Lamberti advised complete revenge in the statement "Cosa fatta capo ha." On Easter morning in 1215, young Buondelmonte came riding across the Ponte Vecchio; as he reached the statue of Mars at the northeast corner of the bridge he was set upon and slain. That bloody moment, according to Dante, was the end of Florentine peace. The names Guelf and Ghibelline, with the old opposition between church and empire, now became engrafted upon the local dissensions between the Guelf Buondelmonti and the Ghibelline Uberti. The quarrel raged thereafter for thirty-three years until in 1248 the Ghibellines achieved a major victory and sent their enemies into exile.

During these thirty-three years the enmity between Guelfs and Ghibellines remained somewhat unfocused until Frederick of Antioch came to Florence as podesta in 1246, intending a feudal organization of Tuscany such as his father had successfully effected in Sicily. In the struggle between the two embattled groups of nobles, the common people, so long overborne and depressed by the haughty aristocrats, seeing in the struggle an opportunity to achieve some measure of self-administration and freedom from the control of outsiders, gradually swung to the support of the Guelfs. It is this persistent self-interest which, from time to time, with the rise of a burgher class and mentality, dictates the increasingly democratic tone of Florentine society. The split between the nobility itself, we note, is one of the many signs of their diminishing power.

With Frederick's support, the Ghibellines gradually assumed control. The Guelfs fled in fear to the strongholds outside the city, leaving their palaces and towers open to the depredations of their Ghibelline enemies supported by Frederick's German horse troops. Razed during the spasmodic battles was the magnificent *palazzo* of the Tosinghi near the Mercato Vecchio and the famous tower of the Adimari near the Baptistry. The Uberti, supported by Frederick's troops, held the city. But out of their failure to consolidate their gains came the first great revolt of the people. It was a momentous occasion, independent of noble support, inaugurating the ten-year period from 1250–60 called the "Primo Popolo."

To the old core of government, consisting of a podesta, leader of the commune and responsible to the nobility, were added the balancing democratic features of a captain of the people, the head of a citizens' army of twenty companies, and a council of ancients, two from each of the six wards of the city. This last feature remains for the history of Florence the essence of that first democratic enterprise.

The new government, dominated by merchant interests, found itself as usual involved in war. By a succession of wars

5

in the first half of the century, Florence had been spreading her control over neighboring cities. Pistoia, Siena, and Pisa all submitted to her rule, and Florence assured herself of a seaport from which to distribute her goods throughout the Mediterranean. During this period Volterra, Poggibonsi, and San Gimignano yielded their independence to the new democracy and marched under its banner of the red lily on a white field. Internally the city was prosperous, and having already in 1235 issued the silver florin, twelve times the value of the denarius, created the gold florin of 1252 having the value of twenty silver florins. These two coins for several hundred years stabilized economic problems of bookkeeping and established the financial genius of Florence. Evidences of a new civic vitality in this period are the building of a fourth bridge over the Arno, the Santa Trinita, in 1252 and the beginning of purely civil architecture in the palace of the people, now the Bargello.

In 1258 the democracy began to show signs of weakness. The Uberti, long head of the Ghibellines, sought aid from Manfred, the natural son of Frederick II, intending to put the city in his hands. Discovered and charged with guilt, many of the plotters lost their heads. In the wild fury the Guelfs destroyed the houses of the Uberti, the Amidei, the Lamberti and others as a revenge upon the Ghibellines who ten years before had treated them in just such a way. The exiles under Farinata degli Uberti fled to Siena, where owing to his organization they won support from Manfred under the leadership of Count Giordano. Toward September, 1260, a Florentine host drawn from every conceivable quarter numbering about 70,000 men moved against Siena. Whether because of the superior cavalry led by Giordano or because of treason in the ranks (as Dante fervently believed), the Florentines were fearfully routed at the battle of Montaperti on September 4. It was a time when, according to Dante, the Arbia ran red with blood. On that day, says Villani, the democracy was broken and destroyed.

The Guelfs were forced to flee from Florence to the near-by city of Lucca. Under Count Guido Novello the conquerors came to re-establish Ghibelline rule. Dante has placed Farinata in hell as an Epicurean, but the pride of city which he and Villani have invested in his character has redeemed him for posterity: when the others of his group would have destroyed Florence he alone defended her, saying that as long as there was life in his body he would defend her with his sword. As a consequence of his brave action the city was saved, but the typical razing of enemy property went on; before the revengeful Ghibellines abated their fury, more than two hundred Guelf properties within and an indefinite number without the city had been torn down.

The Primo Popolo was dead, and for the next six years, during which Farinata died and Dante was born, Florence lay under the oppressive rule of Guido and his German soldiery. In the year of Dante's birth, Charles of Anjou, brother of Louis IX of France, came to defend the papal cause, with the aim of ridding Italy of Manfred and his power. The money for the tremendous undertaking came from the profit-minded Italian bankers who lent it to the French prelates in their war against the now-excommunicated Manfred. On February 26, 1266, the armies met at Benevento, and the exiled Florentine Guelfs who had thrown in their lot with Anjou had the revenge of victory. Manfred died in the battle, his mutilated corpse being identified by the weeping Giordano. His death and his sepulture outside of hallowed ground Dante describes in the third canto of *Purgatorio*, defending the *bello e biondo* Manfred as a contrite Christian in his dying moments, out-witting the excommunication of the church.

With the approach of the French into Tuscany the Guelfs once more took power, accepting Charles as their new podesta, a position which he held through substitutes, dur-ing his absence, until 1280. As for the people, save for a brief moment when it looked as though their rights might be considered, they were no better off than before. Govern-ment remained in the hands of a podesta. No attempt was made to restore to use the office of captain of the people. With the defeat of the German contender Conradin by Angevin forces, the defeat of Ghibellinism became general by 1270. The now highly organized Guelf party completed the destruction of their unfortunate rivals, largely through a system of dispersing Ghibelline wealth into the coffers of the commune, the Guelf party, and of suing individuals within the city. The Guelf party, thus, is clearly a powerful part of city government, sharing with Charles' deputy and coun-cils control of the city.

One feature of the period of Charles' reign in Florence is of tremendous importance. From very early in the thir-teenth century, and even earlier, we have evidence of the formation of guilds. Merchants of foreign cloth, money-changers, wool-dealers among the merchant groups, and a variety of artisan groups appear in documents as already organized into self-protective fraternities or unions. By the time Guido was podesta the greater guilds were seven in number: lawyers, dressers of foreign cloth, money-chang-ers, physicians and apothecaries, wool-manufacturers, silk merchants, and furriers. These were to be the new aris-

8

tocracy of wealth. Shopkeepers and craftsmen of various sorts were organized into at least twenty-five groups from which, as it suited the increasing power of the magnates of industry, various lesser guilds were drawn into alliance with the major guilds. It is these groups, organized first into a body of twelve (five being drawn from the artisan groups) in 1282, then into a body of twenty-one in 1292, which become, through their elected representatives or priors, the central feature of Florentine government.

Such a government waited out the determination of two popes, Gregory X (1271–76) and Nicholas III (1277–80), to diminish the excessive power of Charles of Anjou by restoring some influence to the defeated Ghibellines in Florence. The first failed; Pope Nicholas succeeded up to a point, by inviting Rudolph of Hapsburg to assume the crown of Italy in return for the province of Romagna, and then by sending his nephew Cardinal Latino as peacemaker between Guelfs and Ghibellines. Latino succeeded partly, but the wealthy Guelfs remained powerful leaders of opinion in the city. Charles was out as podesta according to papal deposition, and Rudolph put forth his claim as vicar of Tuscany. Charles, worn out by a succession of disasters (like the massacre of the French occupation troops in the Sicilian Vespers of 1282), died in 1285.

Meanwhile Florence, indifferent to the claims of Rudolph as well as to the unstable compromise government imposed by Cardinal Latino, began to fulfill its economic destiny in a period which Villani could describe as happy and prosperous. It was a period dominated by government in the hands of priors chosen from the various guilds. In short, the wealthy merchants now flourishing in Florence took over the government. With some representation eventually

9

from the minor guilds, the central council of priors became the executive committee, holding office for two months, during which time they lived together as a group and directed policy as an executive unit. The office of podesta continued, but this officer and his councils were balanced out by a captain and his councils acting for the guilds. This limited kind of democracy instituted in the early eighties continued for a decade, pitting its forces against Pisa and Arezzo. It was a period of a steadily rising economy, the beginning of the great fortunes which were to dominate the city hereafter. Socially, historians recall it as a time of festivities, of games and processions, and of clubs, one thousand strong, dedicated to the life of pleasure.

The Ghibellines, still exerting their hostile power throughout Tuscany, precipitated a crisis in Arezzo, to which the Florentines hastily brought their assistance. The nobility of Florence came forward enthusiastically. Dante, then twenty-four years old and immersed in studies, came to take his place in the front ranks, "in much dread, and at the end the greatest gladness." Amerigo di Nerbona, captain under Charles II of Anjou, Vieri de' Cerchi (later to be leader of the White faction), and the great Baron Corso Donati (later leader of the Black faction), all fought ably in the cause of Guelfism in Tuscany. Among the Ghibelline-Aretine enemy were Buonconte of Montefeltro and Guido Novello, who had earlier deported himself so badly in Florence. In the victory of the battle of Campaldino on June 11, 1289, won perhaps because of a precipitous cavalry charge led by Corso and because of the indecision of Novello, Buonconte died. The news of the victory itself, according to Villani, came in a miraculous voice arousing the sleeping priors with the cry, "Arise! Arise! The Aretines

10

are defeated!" Outside the walls of Arezzo, the victorious forces could hold rejoicing games as a gesture of contempt.

The battle against Pisa that followed was less successful, owing to the leadership of the father of Buonconte, Guido of Montefeltro, the subtlest man of war in Italy; and three unhappy campaigns were enough to exhaust the patience of the Florentines. Civic reaction brought about the great political reform under the somewhat mysterious figure of Giano della Bella. Government by priors representing the guilds had not been entirely satisfactory according to Dino Compagni, the historian of these exciting years. The elected officials themselves, being for the most part wealthy and sympathetic to the nobility, worked toward enhancing the position of their class. The instrument against the one-sided power politics of the nobles was a wealthy nobleman himself, a member of the Calimala guild, the democratically inclined Giano, who sought to restrict severely the excesses of his class. His weapon against them was the artisans, the *popolo minuto*, whom he pulled together into a block of nine guilds, with a militia which he added to that of the twelve other guilds. Although Giano, a hotheaded and determined man, was not in the priorate when the great reform called the Ordinances of Justice was passed in January, 1293, he is regarded as its prime instigator and became a prior from February 15 to April 15, 1293, in time to put some of its provisions into effect.

The aim of the Ordinances was, quite simply, to exclude the nobility from holding office and to guarantee that they would keep the peace. Penalties and fines were decided in the event of injury to a common citizen by the upper-class magnates. Especially interesting is the institution of a seventh prior, called the Gonfalonier of Justice, whose task

11

was to carry out the sentences against the magnates decided by the office of the podesta. His task force was made up of 1,000 men, following the banner of their leader, a red cross on a white background. This seventh prior in time became most influential and powerful, and eventually became head of the Florentine Republic.

The Ordinances diverted so much power into the hands of the *popolani* that the *grandi* could complain that their houses might be destroyed if they beat their servants, or if one of their horses flipped a citizen in the face with his tail. On the other hand the vacillating people, zealous to interpret the Ordinances in their own favor, were of a mind to take authority completely into their hands. In the conflict between nobility and people, Giano himself became the victim of a conspiracy and left the city on March 5, 1295. This was the year in which Dante entered into politics by registering himself, in accordance with a provision which allowed it, in the Guild of Physicians and Apothecaries (to which men of intellectual interests were admitted) and became eligible for public office. For the successive seven years until his exile, his name appears in the records of various councils and of the priorate.

While the conflict was brewing, we must take into account Villani's insistence on the vigor of the times: The city boasted up to this point the building known today as the Bargello, then the palace of the people. Now it was to add the great cathedral, Santa Maria del Fiore, and the great Franciscan church of Santa Croce to the already started Dominican church Santa Maria Novella. It was to start construction on the palace of the Signoria, now the Palazzo Vecchio; it was to begin the circuit of the third wall, now occupied by the magnificent avenues which surround the

city. The names of Cimabue and Arnolfo di Cambio in the
arts of painting and architecture were to head the list of the
great artists who grace Florentine culture. Dante in literature was already putting together the work called the *New
Life*, comparing his achievement with that of his friends
and correspondents. And as the millennium came and went
Villani was beginning his history of Florence, the city which
the Pope in the year of the Jubilee called the "fifth element
of the world."

The factional split of the entrenched Guelf party into the
famous Whites and Blacks, thanks to Dino, is easily ex-
plained. In the persons of violent, truculent, proud Corso
Donati, and the moderate, sometimes indecisive Vieri de'
Cerchi, we may see crystallized the hopes of a destitute but
ambitious nobility wanting the return of class to power and
those of a less well organized citizenry intent upon the independence of the city, but more urgently wishing to keep the
advantages guaranteed by the Ordinances of Justice. In its
simplest form the quarrel was social and familial; historically it may have been a family quarrel imported from
Pistoia, a city subject to Florence, but politically the conflict is one of power between two rival leaders, complicated
by the connivance of Corso to throw Florence into the
hands of Boniface VIII and reap for himself and his clan
control of the city.

Clashes and quarrels between the two factions brought
matters to a head in the year of the Jubilee. The Donati
were supported by the Pope, and the Cerchi, in control of
the government, determined to preserve the city from the
Pope's domination. On June 15, 1300, Dante became prior,
and hence was in office when Boniface's emissary, Cardinal
Matteo d' Acquasparta, arrived to bring pressure on the

Whites in power; and during the time of a new outbreak between Blacks and Whites, his priorate took the extreme measure of sending out of the city the leaders of the factions, Corso and his own friend Guido among them. Boniface, however, had laid his plans with Corso and with the brother of Philip of France, Charles of Valois, who was to come to Florence as peacemaker.

Boniface, having failed through embassies both to and from Florence to win the submission of the city, confirmed his plans. On November 1, 1301, Charles of Valois came to Florence at the head of twelve hundred horsemen, an event and time which Dante was to remember with bitterness in the *Divine Comedy*. Deception followed deception, until Corso Donati himself came back from exile to the city, intent upon plunder, while the Judas Charles fattened on gold. The Whites suffered banishment and appropriation of properties. Dante, because he had been an enemy of Boniface and a prior during some of the altercations, was ruined; an exile for the rest of his days, he was yet blessed with the rare capacity for turning his suffering into the greatest poem of its kind the world has ever seen.

The Black victory in Florence bred of itself split allegiances, and Corso found himself embattled against his jealous colleagues; in 1308 he met his death at the hands of paid Catalan mercenaries. His plans had been grandiose: nothing less than lordship in Florence and the abolition of the Ordinances of Justice. Virtually deserted by his friends and supporters in his last hour and disabled by gout, he was taken as he fled out the Porta alla Croce and pierced by a lance of one of the soldiers. Dino himself can hardly conceal his admiration for this Florentine Cataline, although they were on opposite sides of the fray. The great

Baron walks through the pages of history with a swagger that casts his contemporaries into shade.

It was an unhappy decade, one marred by conflict and treachery, but in the middle of it was born that poet greatest after Dante in Italian history, the son of one of Dante's companions in exile. The companion in suffering was named Francesco di Petracco. His son became the famous Petrarch. Whether because he was made weary by the memory of his father's unjust treatment, or because he felt himself a citizen of a larger kingdom, he set foot—and then briefly—in his father's city only when he was himself a middle-aged man and already an established poet and scholar.

The decade that began in 1310 has been illuminated for us by Dante himself in his passionate hopes for a Roman Empire united under a single ideal ruler. The man he hailed was Henry of Luxembourg, come to Italy to fill the seat which had been vacant in the Garden of the Empire. Whether we see him through Dante's eyes or through the pages of history he glows with the luster of a hero. Destined for defeat and an inglorious end, he yet came to infuse life into the moribund dream of a restored Empire. For the better part of three years he sought to subdue the various communes of northern Italy, but Florence, somehow groping steadily toward a more complete autonomy, resisted his attempts, and led a concerted campaign against him.

On the occasion of his advent and during his fateful Italian sojourn, Dante wrote three letters to Henry hailing him as the "Lamb of God," urging him to take up the fight directly against the Florentine vipers, and cursing the wicked opposition of the city. Florence had made provisions, rushing to completion parts of the third wall, making alliances with near-by cities, adding mounted horsemen to its militia; but in 1312 the city could rejoice that Henry's planned attack upon her had been halted by rain and disease and by Florence's own indomitable courage and overwhelming numbers in the face of Henry's presence just a few miles outside her eastern gate. Within the year, on August 24, 1313, Henry died at Buonconvento, his memorial that of admiration from history, and the fact that his name is linked with Dante's highest aspiration for an impossible goal. Italy, Dante will say, was not ready to be set upon the straight path by Henry. He had come to no avail. But his reward is a place in the empyrean among the blessed.

Boccaccio was born in this decade, in the year 1313. About this time Dante had finished in all likelihood his defense of the principle of empire, and was well into the great vision which his disaffected spirit would convert into the high poetry of sublimated hope.

Henry was not long dead when Florence found itself embroiled with Ghibelline Pisa, now protected by one of Henry's lieutenants, Uguccione della Faggiuola, long an enemy of the city. By 1314 he was undisputed dictator of Pisa and then of Lucca. Florence, for protection, had in the previous year taken Robert of Naples as overlord; but even with preparation it suffered the disastrous rout of Montecatini on August 29, 1315. Uguccione found his position threatened and was finally deposed by one of his own men, Castruccio, who became the leader of Ghibellinism against Guelf Florence. Amidst the threats which Castruccio posed, Florence revived the office of captain of the people, and redefined the office of podesta, signs of a characteristic move again toward self-determination. But defeat at Castruccio's hands at Altopascio in September, 1325, forced the city again into the system of an overlord, this time Robert's son, Charles of Calabria, to whom was granted enormous powers and a yearly stipend of 200,000 gold florins.

Charles did nothing to forward Florentine hopes. On the contrary he demoralized the city administration and drained its treasury. To the great relief of the city, his death occurred almost simultaneously with that of Castruccio in 1328, and the city was once more free to make choices necessary to its vitality. For Charles, Florence put on a show of mourning, but according to Coppo Stefani, "for the little good the Florentines got of him, it was very different in their hearts."

Constitutional reform naturally followed in an effort to offset what must be seen as a persistent drift toward oligarchy. The complaint from both Dino Compagni and Villani that the selection of priors from the guilds, always dominated by the more powerful clique, was abused on every side must be taken to be the truth. To offset the domination by the guilds, reform called for nomination and appointment of priors on a new and complicated system by which the names of those eligible for office were first screened and voted upon, and then selected by lot as vacancies occurred. The records of history, confirmed by the testimony of Villani, make it only too clear that the selections as always coincided with the desires of the new rich or *popolo grasso*. Still, the system of councils was considerably simplified to one each for the podesta and the captain of the people. A cabinet of advisers was made up of 12 "good men" and the 16 captains of the military companies. The captain's council, called the Council of the People, numbered 300. Their function was to receive proposals for consideration from the central government, and if they ap-

17

proved them to pass them on to the Council of the Commune, the podesta's group numbering 250.

In the fourteen years or so after the death of Castruccio, when Florence was once again under the guidance of its burgher government, she set out to attain the goal of complete domination in Tuscany. With Castruccio out of the way the city quickly brought Pistoia under its domination, but Lucca, the desired prize, eluded Florence's control. Lucca itself, no longer under the protection of its lord, was sought by many, and as a matter of fact changed hands a number of times during the thirties. Florence attempted to buy the city from Mastino della Scala of Verona while Pisa was simultaneously, by force and by money, stealing the prize. In 1342, Lucca became the Pisan prize, and Florence who had waited so long, negotiated, and fought, found herself the victim of a series of betrayals. In this year, in a desperate measure Florence invited Walter de Brienne, duke of Athens and kin by marriage to the house of Anjou, to become first, captain in charge of military affairs, and soon afterward, overlord.

These years up to the time of the infamous Walter were hailed by Villani as some of the most tranquil since the turn of the century, although it is difficult to credit this. Many fires took place as usual, and the great flood of 1333 swept away the bridges. The statute of Mars which had stood at the foot of the Ponte Vecchio fell into the river, an evil omen for the city. Disease took many lives—first an attack of pox in 1335 and then the dread mortality of 1340, when 15,000 persons died within the city alone. But art was being carried on: in 1330, Andrea Pisano was making the first set of doors for the Baptistry, according to Vasari, on the designs of Giotto. The tower of the Badia, the lower part of it attributed to Arnolfo, was completed. Villani himself was superintendent for the Calimala guild of the improvements of San Giovanni. The San Frediano gate was begun in 1333, and the following year Giotto was superintendent of the works connected with the cathedral, and was himself entrusted with the design and construction of the famous tower that bears his name. He was, too, in charge of the completion of walls and fortifications as city architect, although he was already an old man of seventy at the time.

In 1337 the old pilasters of Orsanmichele were replaced by sturdier ones, and plans were made for the filling of the tabernacles with images of saints sacred to the various guilds. An upper story was planned for the storage of grain, responsibility for the building being assigned to the silk guild. In its special way, the building is a gem, perhaps *the* gem of Florence. We remember that while its construction and interior were the work of the fourteenth century, the statues in the niches are the work of sculptors mainly of the fifteenth century, a roll call of honor: Donatello, Nanni di Banco, Luca della Robbia, Ghiberti, and Michelozzo.

Walter de Brienne was brought to power by the wealthy trading companies, who hoped to stave off bankruptcy with the aid of this chosen tool. Florence was already in the process of financial collapse owing to the depletions of war and the overextension of loans on foreign soil. Walter, however, was guided by self-interest. He was incapable of pleasing any level of the citizenry, and by early 1343 a conspiracy was crystallized against him from all classes. Within the space of a year, the man who had been carried on the shoulders of his admirers in triumph into the Palace of the Priors found himself barricaded within it accompanied by his hastily summoned four hundred soldiers. Not only had the Duke injured the financial nerve of the city; he had shocked a people inured to much that was beastly and cruel by tortures and punishments such as they had never seen.

He had successfully weakened the priorate by depriving them of effective powers, and ruled as a despot by means of his paid soldiery. A battle in the Piazza della Signoria put the soldiers to flight on July 26, 1343. The Duke and his soldiers, with his police official and son, and a friend of the Visdomini family, short of food, remained in their bastion until August 1, when, with the aid of Sienese arbiters and a hastily formed group of fourteen advisers, an agreement was reached. Three hostages who were left behind met a cruel fate. Two of them were dismembered and torn to bits in an ecstasy of mob madness that ended in cannibalism. On August 6, when the fury had abated, Walter de Brienne was given safe conduct over the Ponte alla Carraia and out the San Niccolò gate, and the council of fourteen took over the government.

The priorate was brought back, this time twelve in number. The city was divided into quarters. The Ordinances of Justice were abolished, and thus the *grandi* became eligible for seats in the central committee of government. This was intolerable to the people, and on September 24, less than two months after the Duke had been banished, a series of street fights between the rich magnates and the people brought the magnates down in skirmishes along the Ponte Vecchio, the Ponte alla Carraia, and the Via dei Bardi. The changes effected in the immediate popular reform limited the number of priors to eight members of the people plus the Gonfalonier of Justice, and stripped the seven major guilds

of their control of the priorate by distributing membership
more securely among the minor guilds. The wealthy bankers, stripped of power and influence, could not stave off the
collapse of their banks, and by 1346 were ruined.

To add to the difficulties before the new government of
the people, famine was widespread as a result of a bad
series of crops; and in 1348 the dreaded Black Plague or
Black Death struck with full fury. The full horror of the
Plague in 1348, lasting from April to September, can
hardly be appreciated. It spread with fearful rapidity from
the East, leaping from island to island, thence to Sicily and
Sardinia, Corsica and Elba, and thence by Genoese ships
to the mainland. Two out of three persons died, among
them the Florentine painter Bernardo Daddi and the great
historian Giovanni Villani. To him we owe a horrifying
description of the ravages and consequences of the disease.
Even more famous and more minutely detailed is the introduction to Boccaccio's *Decameron* which supplies the grim
motive for its often lightsome tales. These tales, we recall,
are told by a group of young people who have fled to the
hills outside of Florence for their ten days of feasting,
gaiety, and storytelling.

All the chronicles attest a collapse of moral fiber during
this time, a slackening of will, an indifference to the pressing needs of the time. Two very great works of art, however, among many fine ones, were the direct result of the
Plague. The captains of the Company of St. Michael in the
Garden summoned Orcagna to make a tabernacle for the
miraculous picture of the Virgin in 1349, a work which
was to occupy him for the next ten years. The other work,
the Spanish Chapel by Fra Jacopo Talenti, with its frescoes

by Andrea da Firenze, financed by a grateful Buonamico Guidalotti and directed by Fra Jacopo Passavanti, was completed by the middle fifties.

One remarkable feature of this third quarter of the fourteenth century is the steady complaint that the lowest class of men in the state (and the longest shut out from self-government) were bent on obtaining public office. It is a cry we hear from Matteo Villani, from Boccaccio, and eventually from Matteo's son Filippo in his continuation of the history his father was writing. It is a fact that from 1343 to 1382 shopkeepers and artisans managed to maintain some hand in government, a remarkable experiment in democracy which was never again to take place. The tests which the republic faced it managed well enough. Committed to expansion, it continued to reaffirm its control over the cities of Tuscany. When in 1351, Giovanni Visconti, archbishop of Milan, attempted to extend his power from Lombardy to Tuscany with the aid of widely scattered Ghibellines, Florence staved off his ambitions over a two-year period of debilitating war.

Florence, as well as her enemies, was employing mercenaries to fight its battles, a sad commentary on the weakened military strength which had resulted from a gradual loss of an aristocratic militia, traditionally fighters for the commune. Organized into companies, they became oppressors and masters rather than servants, demanding ransom, laying waste the countryside when they were not engaged in war. The company of the German Guarnieri in the forties, and that of the Frenchman Fra Moriale and the Count of Lando in the fifties, bled the countryside, extorting tremendous sums of money from various cities.

One fact of importance the decade of the fifties demonstrated, namely that the empire was dead: when Charles of Luxembourg, grandson of Dante's Henry VII, with the approval of the Pope in Avignon came to Italy in 1355—the ambassador in this situation was Boccaccio—the Florentines paid him off in florins and prevented his entry into the city. A subsequent visit to Italy in 1368 in support of Pope Urban V proved even more decisively that the empire was defunct.

In the latter part of the fifties quarrels with Pisa over the taxation of Florentine goods passing through that port led to graver disagreements and finally to a series of wars conducted at great costs to both sides, since the soldiers hired first from the English mercenaries and then from the Germans were a great expense. The original issues were obliterated by purely territorial questions until 1364 when, under Galeotto Malatesta, the Florentines firmly defeated the Pisan army, at that time under the command of the famous English mercenary John Hawkwood. The prisoners of war performed the humiliating rite of paying a poll tax as they came through the city gate, and then of kissing the Marzocco, the stone lion which stood in the Piazza della Signoria as a symbol of Florentine might. They were later put to work on the so-called roof of the Pisans which used to stand across the Piazza from the *palazzo*. The war was won, but at great price. For a while at least, a lesson was learned that wars cannot be carried on indefinitely. When Urban V, bringing the papacy back to Rome in 1367, urged Florence to join a league against Bernabo Visconti, Chaucer's "God of delight and Scourge of Lombardy," the city refused. But when in 1369, Bernabo declared himself vicar in Tuscany, Florence was forced again into war on the side of the papacy, this time fighting against Hawkwood who had shifted his allegiances to Bernabo Visconti. The Florentines paid off Hawkwood on the terms that he should not molest Florentine territory, and eventually under pressure of expedience they hired him to fight on the side of the commune against papal control itself.

This rebellion of Florence, the fairest daughter, against her mother, Rome, is explicable if we remember that with the return of the papacy to Italy there came into existence a large but unstable state under the aegis of Cardinal Albornoz. Under the chancellorship of Coluccio Salutati, the author of many letters and treatises in the cause of liberty against an overwhelming tyranny, Florence successfully staved off papal domination under the leadership of a group of eight called I Otto della Guerra, or more popularly I Otto Santi, so enthusiastically did the Florentines take the new war to their hearts from 1375 to 1378, that is, until the death of Gregory XI in the latter year.

One reason for the popularity of the war against the papacy was democratic antipathy toward the brand of Guelfism which had steadily been growing in Florence, a political consensus identifiable with fidelity to the papacy. Naked hatred had been brewing for some time anyway against the Guelf party and its captains, the aristocratic corps that had over some generations aimed to usurp the powers of the democratic city administration, and which little by little had become a powerful organization.

The captains, in existence since 1267, had in the days following the Black Death taken upon themselves the power to define what Guelfism was. In more precise terms, from 1358 on they had tainted with the name of Ghibellinism those whom they deemed ineligible for public office. They could and did proscribe a number of citizens under a system of "admonishments." In this simple way the Guelf party under its captains became a governing body outside the constitutional framework of the city.

In the battle against Pope Gregory, Sacchetti's Pope Guastamondo, the party hesitated to strike against the Eight Saints. But when it appraised public sentiment and found its resolve, it struck for power on June 24, 1378, by seizing the Palace of the Priors and the city government. In office as the banner-bearer of justice was Salvestro de' Medici, an enemy of the Guelf party. He had during the previous week urged the reinstitution of the Ordinances of Justice against the rising power of the *grandi* and suggested that the "admonishments" be more strictly limited. The refusal by the priorate to give him support led to a direct appeal to the people; as the tension over the issue of civic control increased, the lower guilds went raging through the city firing the houses of Lapo di Castiglionchio, the Buondelmonti, the Pazzi, the Strozzi, and the Albizzi, leaders among the hated Guelf party. The riot spread even to the southern part of the city, around the Porta Romana and San Frediano.

By St. John's Day, the first phase of the revolution was over, the hated laws of the Guelf party were annulled, the "admonished" were restored to responsible citizenship, and the leaders of the opposition were sent into exile. Salvestro passed out of office, his place being taken by Luigi Guicciardini. The poet Sacchetti could hail him in June, in a pun upon his name, as *Salvator mundi*, as a just Cato and a new Fabricius. In September, Sacchetti could rejoice that the revolution was over and government was in the hands of the moderates.

The new priorate under Guicciardini had trouble of its

own. Popular discontent had spread down to the long-disenfranchised masses of workers without whom the industry and wealth of Florence were impossible, the *popolo minuto*. They had had a brief moment of recognition as far back as 1343 under Walter de Brienne, a recognition lost when the Duke was deposed. From Walter's reign came the name Ciompi, a distortion of the French word *compère*. The Ciompi were largely wool-washers and -combers, and it is their part in the revolution which has given the popular uprising beginning in July, 1378, the name Ciompi Revolt.

Ever since the loss of their small power under Walter de Brienne, the lower-class workers were under a suppression deep and final. They were forbidden to meet in groups of more than ten. Placed on proscribed lists, they were prevented from working. They were unable to organize themselves into a guild or to arbitrate the terms of their own employment. Now in July, meeting secretly and then acting under the instigation of Salvestro, the Ciompi streamed into the Piazza della Signoria to make their wishes clear. They demanded the right to form a guild and to have a place in the government.

For two days the crowd raged, burning the houses of the rich and seizing the Palace of the Podesta. On July 22 under the leadership of a barelegged wool-comber named Michele di Lando carrying in his hand the banner of justice taken from the house of the Ganfalonier of Justice, the people took over the deserted Signoria. Immediately Michele was declared Gonfalonier and lord of the city. Under his leadership there came into existence immediately not one guild but three: one for dyers, one for garment-makers, and one for wool-workers. Under his guidance the people elected a new priorate which included a generous representation from the hitherto disenfranchised groups.

The amount of direct control which Michele was able to exert was limited. When the end of his term drew near and the mobs, denied work by their revengeful employers, were still demonstrating in the Piazza della Signoria, with sword in hand he rode on horseback through the city calling upon the guild captains to put down any radical action. This was the last day of his office, and on the next day Michele was able to hand over a reasonably tranquil city to his successor.

Under his successor the Ciompi guild was eliminated, but the other two guilds survived. We can say of the hectic summer of 1378 that the minor guilds, thus increased, made a substantial addition to democratic government. The Guelf party as a power was dead and so were the radical Ciompi, although in the next several years conspiracies on the part of exiles to connive for power appeared with regularity.

In one plot involving exiles in Padua, Gianozzo Sacchetti, brother of the poet, lost his head not long after his brother Franco had praised the new government for restoring all good men to brotherhood. In another more critical plot, the demagogues Giorgio Scali and Tommaso Strozzi, magnate leaders of the city, precipitated a crisis which led to the death of the one and the banishment of the other.

In the inevitable reform of 1382 the merchants profited. Backed by Hawkwood and his men, on January 21 a selected committee abolished the workers' guilds, and the major guilds regained the preponderance of power in a triumph for the oligarchical principle, a victory which it was to hammer out permanently in a greater and greater merchant control. The democratic principle in Florence was dead. Ahead lay further reforms, but always those which strengthened the rule of the powerful and rich merchant class. Ahead lay the long war (1390–1402) with the viper of Milan, Gian Galeazzo Visconti, from whom the city was saved by the plague which took his life. And in the next quarter-century lay the rise of the family that was to dominate the Renascence, the Medici.

Behind, hidden by the tissue of politics, Petrarch and Boccaccio had died (1374 and 1375), leaving behind an intellectual inheritance which was to bear fruit in the leadership of Coluccio Salutati, politician and scholar (1331–1406), and Luigi Marsigli (d.1394), the Augustinian who attracted a whole generation of young scholars to him. Established in the year of Dante's death (1321), the University of Florence was to have a stormy and uneven progress. Yet in 1373, Boccaccio became its first lecturer on Dante, and in 1396 the study of Greek, under Manuel Chrysoloras, became a part of the curriculum.

Behind, too, lay the foundation of the great churches, the great civic buildings, the great gates of the third circle of walls. Dead were the great artists who had flournshed in the city or who had worked under its protection: Arnolfo, Cimabue, Giotto, Andrea Pisano, Orcagna, and a host of followers.

A great age had come to an end, and a perhaps greater one was rapidly coming into existence. Ahead lay new developments for humane letters and political writing, for art and for sculpture. The banker Palla Strozzi and the merchant Niccolò Niccoli would promote humanistic studies in Florence. The reform of the university was to make possible a great humanist like Leonardo Bruni. The next age would see the great architects and sculptors Brunelleschi

(1377–1446), Donatello (1386–1466), and Ghiberti (1378–1455); it would produce the painters Masaccio (1401–28) and Fra Angelico (1387–1455). But Sacchetti's *Canzoni* on the death of Petrarch and Boccaccio are the dirges of the century just passed and in fact its closing signatures.

2. *Within Her Ancient Walls*

LOCATED ON TWO SIDES of the Arno River and built on the plateaus which form on either side of it, the city of Florence occupies an enviable geographic position. Not only does it control the route westward to Pisa and the sea; it also sits astride an important route to Rome, some 140 miles to the south. Indeed, from whatever point of the compass one looks upon it, it is a point of confluence on the plains.

This location has the advantage also of being scenically very beautiful. To the northeast rise the wooded hills preliminary to the Apennines. To the south lie the vineyard-covered Chianti Hills. West and north extend the fertile plains rich in orchards and vines. In a matter of minutes the traveler can make his way up and out of the city to one of the promontories from which the city may be viewed: northward up the villa-bedecked slopes lies the ancient city of Fiesole; south and west up the Viale dei Colli, above verdant garden areas, sits the wide Piazzale Michelangelo; to the west of it, the magnificent Fort Belvedere designed and built by Buontalenti for Ferdinand I in 1590. The beauty of the site is enough to blind the viewer to the incredible heat of summer and the damp, penetrating cold of winter. The other seasons are the seasons of flowers, and it is these that the visitor remembers.

The city familiar to Dante and, before him, to his ancestor Cacciaguida was situated primarily "between Mars

and the Baptist," that is to say, between its southern border
on the Arno and its northern limit just beyond the Baptistry. This area, still called "the center," had been girded
from the last years of the eighth century by an ancient wall,
and occupied a space not essentially different from that
of the ancient Roman settlement which Dante and his contemporaries believed came into existence through the good
offices of Julius Caesar. Its shape was that of the Roman
camp, a square with a measurement in excess of five hundred yards on each side, the sides oriented to the points of
the compass. This area was crossed from north to south
and from east to west by the two main streets which divided
the city into quarters. For each of the quarters there was a
gate (Del Vescovo on the north, San Brancazio on the west,
Santa Maria on the south, and San Piero on the east), with
smaller entrances, six in number, at convenient locations in
the wall. At the crossing of the main streets, in the fashion
of a Roman forum, lay the Old Market, occupying the site
of the present Piazza della Republica. At the opening of the
Porta Santa Maria there was, fording the Arno, the bridge
which, many times reconstructed, came to be called the
Old Bridge or Ponte Vecchio.

Within the most ancient walls over the course of centuries up to the twelfth century the old Roman baths,
temples, theaters, and civic buildings gradually crumbled
away. Gardens and fields took over amid the rubble, and
Roman Florence gradually disappeared from the earth.
We know from excavations by archaeologists that there was
an amphitheater for games in the eastern suburb, just beyond the wall, on the site of the present Piazza Peruzzi, and
that the interior of the city contained baths, temples, and an
aqueduct. Far from being a thriving community up to this

31

time, the old town owed its existence chiefly to its position on the river, being a way station, so to speak, on the road to Rome.

Outside the walls on the north there was a church, San Lorenzo, a vastly more simple structure than the one now standing, dedicated by the great Bishop Ambrose of Milan, in the year 393 A.D. In this year too, Ambrose consecrated an early bishop of Florence, one Zenobius. This date marks in effect the end of paganism in Tuscany. San Lorenzo remained the seat of the bishop until the seventh century, when the newly built Baptistry and church of San Giovanni, close inside the north wall and a little to the east, became the episcopal church; to the west of it was built the bishop's residence.

The rapidly growing city very soon began to overflow the confinement of the old wall. Various suburbs sprang up along the main roads leading from the principal gates. The spilling over of the populace into the suburbs outside the first wall necessitated the construction of a second wall to contain and to protect the new neighborhoods which by the middle of the twelfth century had begun to proliferate on all sides of the old center.

This second wall, about 1172, enclosed almost three times the area of the original city and extended the practical control of the Florentine Commune across the Arno. By the time of Dante's youth and the young adulthood of Villani, history had repeated itself. The growth of industry had continued to swell the population of Florence. Outside the second wall more than ten other suburbs had sprung up along the gates, now twelve in number, leading from the city, and these were constantly exposed to attack in the shifting political and martial affairs of the time.

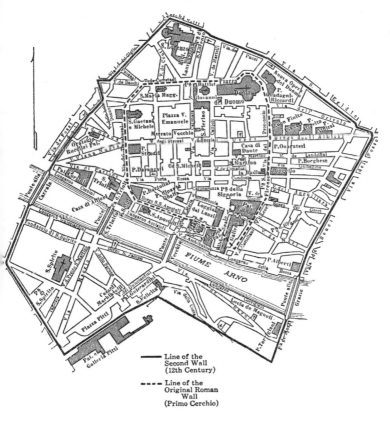

Florence, showing its two inner walls
and the leading public buildings.

From Ferdinand Schevill, *History of Florence* (New York, 1961)

33

Florence

In 1284 when Dante was barely twenty and his city was in the flush of energy signalized by the control of the twenty-one guilds over the affairs of the city, a third wall was initiated. By this time the first wall had been for the most part removed, although signs of it still reminded the thoughtful of the tradition of Rome to which the city belonged. Now as the still standing second wall, pierced by more and more gates, was superseded by a third, a person could feel a mingled pride in the rapid growth of an exciting city, and dismay at the loss of the old ways. Dante did not live to see the completion of the third wall in 1327–28 under the supervision of Villani. It is a truly amazing picture that the latter presents to us of a city surrounded by a great wall almost forty feet high and six feet thick encompassing an area of about five miles. This great wall, pierced by nine gates on the north side of the river and by six on the south, was capped by some seventy-three towers spaced at four-hundred-foot intervals. The entire wall was itself surrounded by a moat which served as one of the means of defense. The space occupied by the great wall is now of course a great circuit of avenues which encompass the city of Florence. Remaining are a few of the gates and some small sections of the wall south of the Arno reminding us of the original structure. The existent Porta Romana manages still to convey something of the fortress-like view the enemy must have had of a virtually impregnable city snug behind its walls.

Florence was, by the time of the third wall, a thriving and bustling commercial city well organized into major, minor, and "middle" guilds; it was a receiving center for goods from far-off places, principally in the wool trade. We can imagine the continuous business at the gates where officials established values with their weights and measures. In the vicinity of the gates there would be considerable activity around the wells and horse troughs maintained by the people of the district for watering animals. The wide road-beds on either side of the walls would, on occasion, be crowded with the caravans waiting either to go out or to come in.

Dante did not live to see the completion of the third wall, but it was during his exile that the hasty ramparts and trenchwork were constructed between the Porta San Gallo and the Porta alla Croce, and from there to the Arno in 1310 when the advent of Henry VII posed a threat to the city.

This was the thrice-circled city coming into a new and exciting existence while Dante, who saw the beginnings of the new in the cathedral, the third wall, and the construction of the Palazzo della Signoria in the years before his exile, remained outcast from his beloved homeland. A source of much of his anguish was the memory of a city already old in tradition, the very names of the streets recalling for him his city's turbulent history.

First among the structures dear to his memory were the hundred or so churches, great and small, distributed among the fifty-odd parishes of the city. Not far from the cathedral he would have seen Santa Maria Maggiore (929–64), especially dear to him because his much-admired teacher, the statesman of Florence, Brunetto Latini, was buried there in 1294. West along the Via Cerratani and south onto the present Via Tornabuoni, in the piazza Santa Trinita where the feud between the Blacks and Whites first drew blood, stood the church Santa Trinita, where his friend and fellow prior, the historian Dino Compagni, argued passionately for peace in June, 1301, and in which Compagni was to be laid to rest in 1324. With him Dante shared in his early manhood one of the most exciting periods of Florentine history.

Not far from here the little church Santi Apostoli (1075) stands on the street which still bears the name. This was the church which, according to Vasari, served as a model in small for Brunelleschi in his reconstructions of San Lorenzo and Santo Spirito. This was the church in which there were preserved stones brought from the Holy Land by Pazza di Ranieri de' Pazzi upon his return from the Crusade of 1088. Supposedly founded by Charlemagne, it would qualify as one of the oldest existing churches in Florence after the Baptistry.

For the area around Dante's own house in the southeast quadrant of the city there was the familiar church of San Remigio (1040), apparently founded as a hospice for French pilgrims on their way to Rome. Here, according to Vasari, Orcagna executed paintings now unfortunately lost. Not far from San Remigio was the church of San Firenze (1174), like all the ancient churches facing to the east, and that of St. Apollinare (1065), no longer standing. This church, too, was richly decorated by Andrea Orcagna and his brother Bernardo when it was rebuilt in the fourteenth century. Outside the east gate of San Piero was the church San Pier Maggiore (969) rich in legend of St. Zenobius. Here in the Benedictine convent of the church each new archbishop of the city performed a ritual marriage between himself and the abbess as a symbolic representation of the new union with Florence.

On the north outside the Porta del Vescovo there was the most ancient church of Florence, the Basilica of San Lorenzo (393) consecrated by St. Ambrose, bishop of Milan, as he fled before the approach of Emperor Eugenius. In its subsequent history it came to be regarded as the *"caput ecclesie florentine"*; the same claim was made for it in 1191, then in 1225 under Pope Honorius III, and again in 1276 by Pope John XXI. Outside the Porta San Brancazio on the west was the church of that name (929–64), no longer in existence.

Across the river, the heart of Oltrarno was made up of three suburbs. To the southwest was San Jacopo with the twelfth-century church of the same name for which Brunelleschi, according to Vasari, built the cupola as an experiment before building the great dome of the cathedral. Straight south on the present Via de' Guicciardini is the suburb containing the old church Santa Felicita built upon the site of a fifth-century Christian oratory and cemetery, presently containing the beautiful Deposition by Pontormo. Straight south and just beyond the Pitti palace is the church of San Felice, with its old monastery and a modest façade by Michelozzo. On this street Machiavelli once lived, wrote, and died (1469–1527). To the southeast of the bridge lies the third suburb, which once contained the church of Santa Maria sopr' Arno, no longer existing, and San Giorgio, much modified in appearance. These three suburbs were included within the city in 1260 when the walls had to be extended to encompass the burgeoning population south of the Arno.

The great churches which today we see silhouetted against the sky, Santo Spirito and Santa Maria del Carmine, came into existence shortly after Dante's birth in 1269 and

1268, respectively. Santo Spirito, once a modest church with two cloisters, as designed and built by Brunelleschi in the early fifteenth century, was destroyed by fire in 1471 and rebuilt according to his designs. The original convent contained hostels, refectory, and hospital, but its greater fame for us rests in its having been an intellectual center for the humanists at the end of the fourteenth century. Here Coluccio Salutati, the chancellor of the Republic from 1375 on, and Luigi Marsigli, the Augustinian friar, conducted discussions of literature and philosophy. In this church was buried Stefano the Florentine (d.1350), the disciple of Giotto, praised by Vasari for attempting the depiction of the human form in a manner far more realistic than that of his master. The church and convent of Santa Maria del Carmine was a modest Carmelite church which gradually became a more lavish edifice toward the end of the thirteenth century. Its fame today is centered in the Brancacci chapel where Masolino, Masaccio, and Lippi painted their famous fresco series.

We could go on proliferating the names of churches large and small within the old walls, each with its special place in the history of Florence and familiar to the poet. Many of them, now gone, have bequeathed their names to places. Of those surviving, the Baptistry and San Miniato outside the city have managed to preserve their essential appearance. Here and there remain façades of several others, which, in the passage of time, have been remodeled and rebuilt. Several demand our attention because of the fact that they played a role in the life of the great poet. San Piero Scheraggio, the eleventh-century church where Dante as prior spoke from the pulpit now preserved in San Leonardo in Arcetri southeast of the city, was razed to make way for the Palazzo della Signoria. We cannot fail to add, too, that church which figures in Dante's personal life: Santa Margherita where Dante's beloved Beatrice and her family worshiped, where the Portinari family were buried, and where, it is thought, Dante was married to Gemma Donati.

A few steps north of San Piero stands the Badia, the ancient monastery whose campanile rang out the canonical hours not only for Dante's time but for that of his ancestor Cacciaguida. Founded in 978 by Willa, the mother of Hugo, margrave of Tuscany, it was at the time the only retreat of its kind. Hugo generously endowed the church with property and donations. When Dante was nineteen the church was rebuilt (in 1284) by the still-new government of priors. The present hexagonal campanile which every visitor to Florence may use as a landmark was constructed in 1330, according to Villani. It is here that Hugo (d.1006) was fittingly buried. His tomb, then an ancient Roman sarcophagus but now more splendid, is the work of the fifteenth-century Mino da Fiesole.

The Badia di San Stefano also demands our interest because it was here that Boccaccio in 1373 began his lectures on the *Divine Comedy*, attended by the Dantean commentator Benvenuto da Imola, and receiving for his services the salary of one hundred gold florins. Among his successors in ths program which he initiated were Antonio Piovano in 1381, and Filippo Villani, nephew of the great chronicler, in 1391.

Some churches in the very heart of the city command more of our attention than others, notably Dante's "beautiful St. John's." The origins of this church are usually ascribed to the seventh century during the Lombard domination of Tuscany. The Baptistry was the cathedral of

Florence until the middle of the eleventh century, having replaced for one reason or another the more ancient San Lorenzo outside the first wall. Adjacent to it on the east was the tenth-century church of Santa Reparata, which more adequately than the Baptistry served the needs of the growing city. As the city continued to swell in the time of Dante and Villani, a new cathedral was planned and carried into execution from the end of the thirteenth century on, on the site of Santa Reparata. The new cathedral was given the name Santa Maria del Fiore, but the people continued to call it Santa Reparata for a considerable length of time.

The Baptistry was in Dante's time a glorious monument. The interior was lined in white and green marble. By 1225 it had received the beautifully executed mosaics of the apse. In 1271 were begun the mosaics which Dante saw during the thirty years it took to complete them. These magnificent designs depicting scenes from Genesis, and from the lives of Joseph, Christ, and John, Dante remembered well enough in exile to incorporate into his great poem. Dante saw too, in 1293, the placing of the new green and white marble around the exterior and the removal of tombs and monuments from around the structure, facts also reported by Villani. Here it was that Dante's close friend Guido Cavalcanti, according to a tale by Boccaccio, contemplated the existence of God. It was here that Dante broke the baptismal font to save the child who was suffocating in one of the apertures. It was to this church that Dante was subsequently invited to return as a penitent, an invitation he scornfully refused.

From their origins in the thirteenth century the Dominican and Franciscan orders spread and established themselves throughout Italy. Their strongholds, respectively, in

Florence are Santa Maria Novella to the west of the second wall, and Santa Croce to the east. By 1221 the Dominicans had a small church in Florence, which in the passage of time accumulated cloisters, dormitories, refectory, library, and bell tower. It became after 1283 the imposing Gothic structure which we now see. Here the nefarious Charles of Valois came in 1301 to promise, in the presence of the priorate, the captain of the people, and the podesta, that he would preserve the peace of Florence. The story of his deception, his connivance with Corso Donati, the rampant plunder of the city, and Charles' abandonment of the city are told with controlled passion by Dino Compagni, who, with Dante, is a historical witness to the betrayal.

Vasari and others attribute the building of the church to two friars, Sisto and Ristoro, but this is a much-debated point. By the middle of the fourteenth century it had acquired part of its marble façade and the characteristic bell tower. The façade which we now see is the design of Alberti (1458). The whole church was reworked and remodeled by Vasari in the sixteenth century. Dissatisfied with what seemed to him the barbaric Gothic style, he had the floor raised, the tombstones destroyed, and the frescoes covered over. Here Boccaccio's young people met on a Tuesday morning in Santa Maria Novella during the Plague in 1348, and here they planned their pleasant escape from the city.

The Franciscan church Santa Croce also dates back to the early days of the thirteenth century. In 1212 a small group of Franciscans had come to Florence. By 1228 they had a small Romanesque church which was enlarged in the subsequent quarter-century. Inadequate in size, the old church was gradually replaced after 1295 under the guidance of the great Arnolfo di Cambio, the designer of the great cathedral Santa Maria del Fiore and the Palazzo della Signoria. Villani tells us that the old church was maintained for worship while the new one was being built, and that the old one was finally torn down in 1336 to make room for the nave and aisles of the greater structure.

The members of the third order of Franciscans, which attracted so many to the vows of humility, poverty, and chastity, used to meet in the Castellani or Sacrament chapel. Was Dante among them as a young man? He would not have seen, of course, the later illustrations from the life of St. Francis which Giotto painted upon the walls of the Bardi chapel, only rediscovered in the middle of the nineteenth century, since he was in exile during the time they were painted.

Of special interest to the time was the privilege of being buried within the properties of the church, under the wings so to speak of the great saint. In the first cloister, designed also by Arnolfo, are tombs dating from 1285, and providing for posterity a kind of record of Dante's age. Subsequently, within the church, among the illustrious dead were to be placed Michelangelo in a tomb designed by Vasari, Leonardo Bruni, and Galileo, among other great men of Florence.

The earliest documents dealing with Santa Reparata are those of the eighth and ninth centuries. Both Giovanni Villani and his brother Matteo report that a church which had been called San Salvatore was changed to Santa Reparata because Florence, in the time of St. Zenobius, scored a victory on her feast day against the assaulting Goths. The year was 407. Whatever the origin of the name, we may have some idea of the appearance of the church from subsequent records, which establish that the church bore a resemblance both to the cathedral at Fiesole and to the Basilica of San Miniato. It had become the cathedral of Florence only after San Giovanni, now the Baptistry, having served as the cathedral, proved too small for the burgeoning population. In the last decade of the thirteenth century, there being a period of peace, the citizenry decided to build a new and larger church upon the old, and to adorn it with marble and sculptures.

The year was 1296. Pisa and Siena were also in the process of raising cathedrals, and something of Florentine rivalry shows in their grandiloquent proclamations: "The Florentine Republic, soaring ever above the conception of the most competent judges, desires that an edifice should be constructed so magnificent in its height and in its beauty that it shall surpass anything of the kind produced in the time of their greatest power by the Greeks and Romans." And again: "Since the highest mark of prudence in a people of noble origin is to proceed in the management of their affairs so that their magnanimity and wisdom may be evinced in their outward acts, we order Arnolfo, headmaster of our commune, to make a design for the renovation of Santa Reparata in a style of magnificence which neither the industry nor the power of man can surpass."

Although the name Santa Reparata was not given up by the people for at least a century, the name of Santa Maria del Fiore was bestowed upon the church at the laying of the foundation. Taxes out of the city treasury as well as money solicited from the pious provided the revenue. The building of the church as we have seen was entrusted to Arnolfo, since he was already an established architect and sculptor, a student of Nicola Pisano (*ca.* 1206–78), who had sculpted the magnificent pulpit for the Baptistry in Pisa.

But financing amidst war and civil disturbance is precarious. Although by the time of his death in the first decade of the fourteenth century Arnolfo had apparently completed some bays (according to Vasari, the three principal tribunes which were under the cupola) and a façade, work came to a halt during the troubled years that followed. Work on the cathedral was intermittent after 1330. Funds were again available from the wool guild, and Giotto became the superintendent of works for the commune and thus of the cathedral in 1334. What he accomplished we cannot know for sure. Upon his death in 1337 he was succeeded by Andrea Pisano (1337–48), the creator of the first set of doors on the Baptistry, then by Francesco Talenti (1349–59), and so on until the year 1378, when the main work on the cathedral was finished and the last section of the old Santa Reparata was demolished.

Arnolfo's façade was brought down in 1358 in order to allow for a more Gothic one under the guidance of Francesco Talenti. The subsequent changes, many feel, have forever destroyed the artistic unity which Arnolfo intended. Be that as it may, the crowning of the cathedral with the marvelous cupola of Brunelleschi is the work of the second and third decades of the fifteenth century. What is Arnolfo's, and what the work and plans of others, is difficult to say. It is probable that the octagon over which Brunelleschi's dome rests was a part of Arnolfo's original plan.

On the northwest was a bell tower which had been used all the while that Giotto's bell tower was being constructed on the southwest from 1334 on. This structure did not come down until 1357.

The foundations for the new tower were laid in July, 1334, and the building could not have gone much beyond the first story with its bas-reliefs when Giotto died and the work was handed on to Andrea Pisano, and then to Francesco Talenti, under whom the three higher stories were completed. The full extent of Giotto's contribution with regard to the ornament is itself not fully known. Andrea seems to have executed a number of the reliefs from designs or cartoons given him by the master.

One of the churches which is a sign both of Florentine practicality and of piety, and which has as bizarre a history as any in Dante's age, is Orsanmichele. In Dante's time it was a grain market, but earlier there had been on this site a church dedicated to St. Michael. In 1239 after the church was destroyed, the site enjoyed various uses until 1284 when a loggia was erected there to serve as a shelter for the grain market. On one of the pillars was painted a Madonna, which very soon became associated with miracles.

"So greatly grew the fame of these miracles," writes Villani, "that folk flocked hither in pilgrimage from all parts of Tuscany at her feasts, bringing various waxen images for the wonders worked, with which a great part of the loggia in front of and around the said figure was filled." So it remained, partly a shrine and mainly a grain market, until one of the savage altercations between the Black and White factions in 1304 during which the Whites were defending themselves stoutly in the area of Orsanmichele. One of the Blacks, Neri Abati, set fire to the houses in the vicinity, starting a major conflagration which destroyed the loggia but not the miraculous image of the Virgin. Houses right down to the Ponte Vecchio were destroyed, and as a result the Cavalcanti family were wiped out and were forced to leave the city.

A new and flimsy loggia of wood was built which lasted

with repairs through the famine of 1329. Finally in 1337 the city administration planned a reconstruction on a grander scale, to include two top floors for the storage of grain. Begun almost immediately, the work went on for another twenty years before the structure could be called reasonably complete. During this time Bernardo Daddi provided a new picture of the Virgin, and Orcagna was commissioned to provide a tabernacle for it. In 1357 the grain market was moved to the Piazza del Grano, and two years later the construction was dedicated as a church. Eventually the spaces between the pillars were closed, from 1366 on.

On each of the pilasters there is a tabernacle in which there was to be placed a figure of the saint revered by the various guilds as their patron. The fourteen niches are presently filled by sculptures of the fifteenth century from the hands of masters like Donatello, Ghiberti, Verrocchio, and Luca della Robbia.

Within is one of the glories of fourteenth-century art, the splendor of the Orcagna tabernacle which we shall describe in the next chapter. The architects whose names we trace in the history of the building are the familiar ones with which we associate the progress and development of the cathedral itself: Francesco Talenti, Benci di Cione, Neri di Fioravante, and Simone Talenti, all prominent in the latter half of the fourteenth century.

In the foregoing we have been looking principally at the building of churches and convents. The thirteenth century is also the age of civic building in Florence. In 1255 the rugged fortress with a tower, the Palazzo del Popolo, was constructed. It is in effect the monument of the Primo

46

Popolo, the first experiment in democracy which, we have seen, lasted the ten years from 1250 to 1260. It was intended as a residence of the captain of the people, the Guelf nobleman whose task it was, with his twenty companies, to defend the interests of the people against the Ghibelline nobility. This building was furthermore intended to house the councils, who had previously used various churches for their meeting places. It was to be some time before the government of the people would have its own building, for in 1260, with the battle of Montaperti, the first democracy was over, and the Palazzo del Popolo became the Palazzo del Podesta.

In spite of the fact that the impulse which brought the Palazzo into existence was essentially democratic, the massive architectural form which it imitated was that of the feudal nobility, namely, the castle. It is a massive square block, its lines broken by the mullioned windows. It is topped by the high battlemented tower and still presents a severe aspect to the onlooker. By 1280 a corresponding block was added to the original, and this was joined to the forepart by colonnades supporting a vaulted portico. The beautiful courtyard between the two sections of the building is one of the glories of medieval architecture. In the first quarter of the fourteenth century upper stories above the porticos were added, and by the middle of the century the splendid staircase which leads up from the courtyard was finished.

Here Dante was summoned to appear in 1302 before the podesta's court to be sentenced; and here, as Dino tells, in 1303, Fulcieri da Calboli, the cruel executor of justice, tortured the Whites who fell into his hands. Here, too, the Ciompi, in their July riot of 1378, wishing to be recognized

47

as a guild with the right of participation in government, destroyed the records of the hated wool guild before they occupied the Palazzo della Signoria.

In the sixteenth century the building became a prison, the name Bargello itself signifying the police official who lived in it. Eventually in the nineteenth century it became a national museum and today it is one of Florence's finest, with sculptures of Donatello, Verrocchio, Della Robbia, Desiderio da Settignano, Mino da Fiesole, Michelangelo, and other geniuses of the Renascence. The magnificent courtyard staircase, by Benci di Cione and Neri di Fiora- vante, and the first-floor loggia comprise one of the most gratifying architectural pleasures of the city.

Off the loggia to the right is the great hall in which the General Council met. It was here that Dante spoke, on September 13, 1301, on behalf of the threatened Ordi- nances of Justice. His physical likeness as well as his spirit is here, as all Dantists know, in the fresco portrait of the youthful poet which Giotto painted in the chapel of the podesta, the room where condemned prisoners passed their final night presumably in prayer. It is this portrait which the Florentine popular poet Antonio Pucci sub- sequently described.

Of the same period as the cathedral is the Palazzo Vec- chio, perhaps the most famous of the civic buildings which originate at the end of the thirteenth century. This building is also the work of Arnolfo di Cambio and may be assigned to the year 1299. When in 1280 and the years thereafter the merchant guilds took over the government of Florence, the actual administration of affairs was the work of the priors acting as an executive body to which even the podesta was henceforth to be responsible. The priors themselves were at this period guild representatives chosen to serve for a period of only two months, during which time they lived together as a group in a rented house. The various councils associated with government met in assigned churches.

From 1290 on the priors were housed in the dwelling belonging to Gherardino de' Cerchi, behind the church of San Procolo. As Villani describes it, because of the contentiousness between the people and the magnates over the choice of priors every two months, those who ruled the city were adjudged unsafe in their dwelling, and a new building was contemplated and planned. The ground chosen for the site of the new building was that formerly occupied by the Uberti houses, Ghibellines and rebels; these houses had some years before been razed to the ground, and a piazza created to assure that they would never be rebuilt.

With some additional property acquired from the Foraboschi family, there was enough space for the new building. Arnolfo, famed for other works in the city, was hired as the architect, and in 1299 the civic monument began to arise, with the special limitation that it not be placed on the hated Uberti land, and that the architect utilize the existing Foraboschi tower in his design. This Arnolfo accomplished, setting the building slightly askew, modeling it, like the Bargello, after a castle or fortress of sorts. He added height to the existing tower and capped it with a battlement. It was completed in three years, at least sufficiently for the government of priors to take up residence there. It is the monument to the second democracy, as the Bargello is the monument to the first. Its bell was installed temporarily outside the building during the first decade of the fourteenth century, and during this same decade the piazza was paved.

49

We can hardly speak of the building's being completed, for it underwent considerable change in the subsequent generations. The platform from which the priors addressed the people was built in 1322. A great door, the work of Andrea Pisano, was added in 1342 to increase the safety of the building by the Duke of Athens during his nefarious regime. This is now gone. Next to the building and joined to it was the residence of the captain of the people, and next to that the residence of the executor of the Ordinances of Justice. Both of these, according to Davidsohn, were incorporated into the *palazzo* in the sixteenth century, along with the building housing the lions back of the *palazzo*. The lions, once the symbol of popular independence, disappeared under the Medici.

We cannot get a clear view of the city without calling to mind that characteristic feature of medieval towns, the towers. The principal aspect of the city seen from afar up until 1250 was that of a forest of tall stone-and-mortar structures erected along the principal arteries of the city right up to the edge of the second wall but centered principally within the first circuit. Taken together with the steeples and campaniles which topped the many churches, tall structures numbered more than 275, the bulk of them towers.

Towers came into existence as a result of crowded conditions of the city which necessitated the use of more and more restricted space. More precisely the towers were the result of the persistently savage vendetta spirit which has marked Italian medieval life. They provided residences for the nobility, but their main function was to provide refuge

50

from enemies during the riots which periodically broke out. The tower came to be the symbol of the great families which from time to time joined together with other families for mutual protection in an association called a *consortería*. The towers were thus a sign of power, of wealth, of race. The nobility vied with each other in more pretentious and higher towers as a means of fighting off marauding rivals. Some of the towers attained a height in excess of 120 *braccia*, or about 230 feet.

By 1250 when for the first time the people managed to gain some share in the government and were more powerful than the oppressive *grandi* class, the nobility, almost without realizing it, were in the process of giving up their control over the city. The tower associations were decimated. By civic enactment the towers were reduced to less than half their original size (50 *braccia*), and the stone salvaged from them was used in part to build the walls on the south side of the Arno.

Since living in the towers proved to be an inconvenience, the great families tended to build more comfortable quarters for themselves alongside their towers. These were houses of wood when it was available, but for the most part were constructed of stone and occasionally of brick. By 1300 the towers had, owing to the advancement of civil law and an increasingly cultural sophistication, lost their function; their bottom floors came to be occupied by stores and shops, and their unused upper stories were now allocated to storage. Nonetheless they have left their mark upon the city, and relics of them are still visible to the questing eye.

Especially numerous around and in the Old Market, among them were the towers of the Ubaldini, the Elisei, the Caponsacchi; in the Borgo Santi Apostoli, that of the Buondelmonti; near the Porta Santa Maria, that of the Amidei; near the Corso, that of the Donati; and in the Via Calzaioli, that of the Adimari. Across the Arno there were the towers of the Frescobaldi family and of the Bardi—all in all a familiar roll call of ancient Florentine history. Remnants are still available for the viewer's eye, among them the Torre della Castagna near Dante's house, the first residence of the priorate of 1282 where the priors gathered in order to escape their enemies.

† † †

Dante laments, in the words of his great-great-grandfather, the luxury that has overtaken the city. The residences of which he speaks were destroyed in the seesawing of political fortune, the Guelfs destroying the habitations of the Ghibellines during their period of ascendancy, and the Ghibellines destroying properties of the Guelfs during theirs. For example, after the battle of Montaperti in 1260, the Ghibellines leveled the houses and towers of their enemy, destroying over one hundred large dwellings and some six hundred smaller ones. Two years earlier the Guelfs had done approximately the same thing to the Ghibellines.

Fire in 1304, set by the Black Guelfs against the Whites, is supposed to have destroyed about seventeen hundred houses, including among them the houses and towers of the great families, those of the Cavalcanti and those of the Gherardini. The houses of the Uberti, we remember, were destroyed to make way for the building of the Palace of the Priors. The houses that came into being after 1270 were for the most part the property of the new moneyed merchant and banking classes, marks of the new wealth which could vaunt itself in sumptuous display.

Some of these have survived the years in one form or another: the Palazzo Mozzi in the Via dei Bardi where Pope Gregory X stayed during the time of the reconciliation of the Guelfs and Ghibellines in 1273; Cardinal Latino, repeating the terms of the reconciliation in a public ceremony, stayed there in 1279 and 1280. And Peter of Anjou, brother of Robert, king of Naples, stayed there in 1314. At the foot of the Ponte Santa Trinita, also on the south side of the Arno, was the Frescobaldi palace, now much restored, where Charles of Anjou, king of Naples, lived in 1273. Both Villani and Compagni speak of this palace as the place where Charles of Valois and his court maintained headquarters in 1301. The piazzas of these two palaces still bear the names of their owners.

Across the river and opposite the church of Santa Trinita is the Spini palace, a great house which once had a tower. It overlooked the river and the bridge, an important factor in the turbulent defensive battles that sprang up from time to time and necessitated manning approaches to the bridge. Charles of Valois, recognizing its strategic importance, also occupied this one in 1301, according to Dino Compagni. Near Santa Trinita was the less pretentious palace of the Gianfigliazzi which also served to guard access to the river.

Noteworthy in the southeast quarter of the city is the Palazzo dei Peruzzi, built on the site of the Roman amphitheater and so possessing a curved front conforming to the ancient line. Robert of Naples stayed there in 1310 on his way back from his coronation at Avignon. There are others of considerable interest, for example that of the Davanzati family, that of the Cerchi, that of the wool guild, that of the Minerbetti, the remains of the Alberti palace now having only the loggia, and that of the Guelf party, all of which bear witness to the new rich cast of society. With their balconies and terraces, their open loggias, their upper stories overhanging the streets (until they were taxed out of existence and finally outlawed), they must have been the ultimate in sumptuous living, without parallel until the grandeur and display of the Renascence.

† † †

Historically a great deal of Florentine vitality is the result of its geographical position on a river, on the main route between Rome and the north. By the time of Dante's birth it had become a tangle of towers and a web of churches and piazzas, of encircling walls and a gradually emerging civic architecture. The bridges are one more evidence of the energy which characterizes the mercantile vitality of Florentine history.

The Ponte Vecchio is Florence's most famous bridge. Every visitor to Florence has walked its length and marveled at the fine display of gold and silver in the shops lining it. A tenth-century record suggests a wooden bridge with stone pilings or pillars. Demolished by a succession of floods in its history, its two fourteenth-century reconstructions were of stone. Villani tells us that the reconstruction by Neri di Fioravante in 1345 produced a bridge thirty-two *braccia* wide (about sixty feet), with a roadway between the shops some sixteen *braccia* wide. This is a considerable advance upon the earlier bridge which had a total width of about twelve *braccia* and was somewhat higher. During this reconstruction the bridge contained forty-three shops, each eight *braccia* wide and mounted on solid arches.

The bridge was not always occupied by gold- and silversmiths. Butchers and meat-venders rented space from the commune for about eighty gold florins a year. Subsequently Cosimo I ordered these vile guilds to be removed, and their space allotted to the more glittering arts. The bridge's fame in the history of Florence of course has to do with that fateful and malevolent Easter morning in 1215 when Buondelmonte was murdered. This calamity Villani attributes to Satan's exercising his evil power through the statue of Mars, so venerated up to this time by the Florentines. This was the only one of Florence's bridges not destroyed by the Germans in 1944, although their demolitions did destroy an area some 650 feet on either side of the bridge, doing virtually irreparable damage to the Borgo San Jacopo and to the Via dei Bardi on the south side of the Arno. Gone too is the gallery-corridor, originally built by Vasari, that spanned the bridge, connecting the Uffizi and Pitti palaces.

The Ponte alla Carraia, the second of the bridges, was built in 1218–20 for the growing commerce between the Borgo Ognissanti and Oltrarno. It was called in its day the "new bridge," to distinguish it from the old. The river here met with the Mugnone, that other river which helped to shape the topography of Florence. At the confluence there was a small island called Sardinia on which the Umiliati had built their fulling mills. Near by were the landing and loading platforms for the barges carrying goods up and down the river. From here upstream as far as the Ponte alle Grazie, from 1283 on, there extended the street called Lungarno between the east and west edges of the second wall.

In 1237 the Ponte Rubaconte was built, named after the then-ruling podesta, Rubaconte da Mandello. This is the bridge which Dante mentions in *Purgatorio* XII. The name that it now bears was derived from the oratory which stood at the north end honoring Our Lady alle Grazie, also venerated as the intercessor in affairs of the heart. The bridge also contained in the fourteenth century various cells for pious female recluses, a strange phenomenon amidst the hubbub of the traffic on the bridge.

The Ponte Santa Trinita was the last of the bridges to be built in this half-century (1252). Once rebuilt by the two friars Sisto and Ristoro who designed Santa Maria Novella, it was destroyed by flood, along with the other bridges, in 1333, was rebuilt by the architects of Santa Reparata in 1346, and then again by Ammanati in 1567–69. In its present state, restored with much civic perturbation after the destruction in 1944, it still qualifies as one of the most graceful bridges in the world, its arches apparently designed after the supports under the four figures of night and day, dawn and twilight in the Medici Chapel of San Lorenzo. The bridge is now adorned by four eighteenth-century statues representing the seasons. After their destruction in 1944 the statues were restored except for the lost head of Spring. The head of Spring, after seventeen years of world-wide advertisement for its return, was discovered in a heap of Arno muck by a dredger operator in October, 1961, and was soon thereafter replaced upon the statue.

In the fourteenth century building continued on all fronts: churches and convents, private dwellings, and civic structures. New landmarks came into existence: the prison for the nobility called Le Stinche, named after a castle of the Cavalcanti taken in 1304. The confraternity of the Misericordia, famed for its selfless labors on behalf of the sick and injured, in 1321 purchased from the Adimari the site of their oratory south of the Baptistry. Sometime in the 1350's the elegant Gothic loggia called the Bigallo was erected on the location of the lion house. The twenty or so lions were transferred to the street behind the Palazzo della Signoria, still called the Street of the Lions. Gothic influence was for the most part limited to church structure, for the *palazzi* continued to develop the traditional architecture, more in keeping with the fortress-like walls of the city. Gothic, which had enjoyed a brief flourishing in the thirteenth century, gradually became subservient to the different demands of this special area of Italy, to its special quality of sun and light, and to its fondness for marble.

One of the structures which still graces the Piazza della Signoria is the famous Loggia dei Priori, now named the Loggia dei Lanzi. The name is derived from the German lancers who under Duke Cosimo were stationed in Florence. Florentines still accept the judgment of Vasari that the loggia was the projected plan of the famous Orcagna. The triple-arched open loggia, which forms the south boundary of the piazza before the Palazzo Vecchio, did not come into existence, however, until sometime in the 1370's and was completed early in the 1380's. It now houses an assortment of fifteenth- and sixteenth-century sculptures.

Dante, Compagni, Villani, and Boccaccio were witnesses to the great changes that shaped the city. Even in Dante's time and from his time on, many of the streets whose names are a record of Florentine history were paved and provided with gutters to carry off the water. Street maintenance was the thorn in the side of the city councils, who had the perennial problem of how to finance the improvement of the streets. The Old Market and the piazza before the Baptistry, the accesses to the bridges, and other important places in the life of the city were paved even in Dante's time. Later, in 1330, the piazza before the Palazzo Vecchio was finally paved.

Formal nomenclature of the streets did not exist until after Dante's time. The streets drew their names, as time passed, from the families who owned the imposing structures on them, or from official residences, or from the artisans whose shops lined them. These names would themselves change when families moved and new families entered the neighborhood, or when the artisans of one guild would exchange shops with the members of another guild. Topography itself had a great deal to do with the naming of the streets, an irregular street having a different name for every jog. Streets might also take their names from places to which they led or which they crossed, or from a near-by landmark like a garden. These streets, narrow by modern standards, yet accommodated throngs of people. Wares were laid out on carts or small platforms, or up against the walls of the various shops, identifiable first by some sign or symbol, usually an animal, and finally in the fourteenth century by a number.

Street life was an exciting spectacle. Political affairs such as the installation of the new priors, or religious celebrations such as processions of pious chanting brothers, offered continuous variety to life. An occasional cortege, the chairs and carriages of the nobility, or horse-drawn carriages might even provide a menace for the people on foot, as Sacchetti indicates in more than one place in his stories. Heralds with their trumpets on occasion summoned the people to hear some special announcement at bridges, at crossroads, and at principal piazzas. And everywhere one could count on the lucrative activities of pickpockets and cutpurses, at the various markets like Orsanmichele, active in their trade although subject to the loss of a hand or a foot if caught. Sacchetti writes that beggars and thieves would swarm to church doors and on special holidays would make trips to near-by cities to capitalize on the feast-day crowds.

The city within its first two walls must have presented, even after the reduction of the height of the towers, a fairly solid façade of a stone forest to one approaching from any quarter. But the city within had a variety and an openness provided by the generally dispersed piazzas outside the churches. Its *palazzi*, although severe in appearance, had terraces and sun porches, and provided for sun and light, at least for the wealthy. But the city was also brightened then, as it is now, by gardens, many of them the property of the wealthy. The third wall was of sufficient amplitude to provide space inside for orchards and gardens, and many of the churches and convents that had sprung up in the thirteenth and early fourteenth centuries had their own orchards and gardens. A certain Durante dei Chiarmontesi, whom Dante mentions scornfully twice in the *Divine Comedy*, had a garden with 3,500 orange and lemon trees. This garden Corso Donati, in the fierce destruction of 1301, leveled to the ground as part of his revenge upon the family.

Dino Compagni could write that Florence had become a city so beautiful with art and architecture that travelers came from afar to see its elegance. Villani could boast of the signs of riches in its splendid houses and imply a comparison with Rome. Antonio Pucci by 1373 could describe Florence in glowing terms as a city of palaces and gardens, each finer than the other. It is this beauty which, in addition to art, has made Florence a beloved city over the years.

These writers were praising their city as a visible entity.

Their views were not distracted by personal feelings about its irritating climate, or about its stormy political history. One's modern impression is not vastly different. Looking down upon Florence from a vantage point, one apprehends what they meant. The city, by virtue of its position on the river and its wide distribution of monuments, gives the impression of a sensible control of space and a virile adaptation to geography. Whether it is or is not the ideal city of the mind that we see as we stand off from it, it is as pleasant and masculine a vista as we can imagine. We feel, as Wordsworth felt looking upon London, a certain calm and serenity which the view seems to imply. Yet an energetic spirit informs the ideal, one aspect of which is the artistic energy which manifests itself in the ornament of the city seen only when we come down from the hill and confront it face to face. It is a beauty seen close up which has made Florence a revered city of treasures; and the history of its art from the time of Dante to that of Boccaccio constitutes a roll call of singular honor: Cimabue, Arnolfo, the various Pisan sculptors, Giotto and his school, Orcagna . . . .

3. Craft and Art

BY THE END of the third quarter of the fourteenth century the ground plan of the great cathedral was complete and the last vestiges of the old church of Santa Reparata were removed from within its walls. Plans for the so-called Loggia dei Lanzi, the triple-arched portico which was intended to form part of the larger design for the improvement of the square, had been projected to be completed in 1382, the year in which the Florentine democracy in a sense expired.

The period in history coming to a close marks the end of the first Italian Renascence in art, in literature, in sculpture, and in architecture. This is not to say that there were not artists at work in these various fields, but only that one great age had paved the way for a new one. There had begun to appear on the threshold of the new those great names which mark the second advance: the architects Brunelleschi, Michelozzo, and Leon Battista Alberti; the sculptors Lorenzo Ghiberti, Donatello, and Luca della Robbia; the painters Fra Angelico and Masaccio, and after them a host of names which comprise a veritable encyclopedia of Florentine painting: Paolo Uccello, Andrea del Castagno, Domenico Veneziano, and Fra Lippo Lippi. They are clearly men of the fifteenth century.

The names we have given are of course the great names of fine art. The distinction between fine and useful art is somewhat artificial when applied to the *trecento*, since the

61

distinction between what was an art and what was a craft was not so finely drawn in those days. Florence's economic development is as a matter of fact the development of the arts *and* the crafts. A common sense of integrity, a common sense of beauty are to be found as much in art as in the crafts: in wrought iron, in shields, in weather vanes, in brackets and hooks on the façades of the buildings. The skills collateral to architecture such as the decoration of houses, the creation of furniture; the use of materials like silks, wools, taffetas, and satins; the use of paintings, tapestries, and the like; even the adornment of the person with precious stones or pearl-encrusted diadems, and the design of clothing, among other things, indicate the interpenetration of the artistic and the practical in Florence.

It is clear that Florentine genius, its art and enterprise, are far from being merely ethereal things created by men divorced from the economic and industrial life of the city or from the intellectual currents of the time. Stone, wood, metal, leather, and iron have been as much the media through which the spirit of art has expressed itself as paint and pigment, and the *palazzi*, bridges, and churches of the city have been as much its real expression. The minor guilds of builders, for example, included sculptors, architects, bricklayers, carpenters, and masons; the guild of doctors and apothecaries included sellers of spice, painters, and booksellers. The guild of the silk merchants included detachments of embroiderers, goldsmiths, and silversmiths. In the days of Florence's most hectic history, art permeated the very fiber of life and was tied in very often with the sale of articles made for the trade. It was not a great age of written theory.

Dante's time and that of Boccaccio were, to be sure,

beginning to develop attitudes toward what we call the "fine arts," but art was not enveloped in mystery nor had it acquired any rarefied vocabulary. Whether the craftsman was at work on iron or gold, the chances are that he was being trained in a variety of disciplines with long apprenticeship, and was prepared to bring to bear upon his work a careful sense of economy and tradition as well as beauty.

Versatility was the characteristic of the age. Arnolfo was a sculptor as well as an architect and a civil engineer. Giotto was a painter, a writer of verse, an architect, and a sculptor. Orcagna was a goldsmith, an architect, a painter, as well as a sculptor. In this range of powers, Dante's age is not different from the age waiting to be born. Although the artists' names are usually associated with a special skill like sculpture or painting, the great ones, like Donatello, Brunelleschi, Michelozzo, and Luca della Robbia dazzle the mind of posterity with the range of their talents in useful as well as fine art. Whatever their favorite medium, each artist evinces the same competitive spirit, ever seeking to widen, by novelty or technique, the intellectual horizons of a burgeoning city. The city itself, through the major guilds which commissioned and paid for work of all kinds on civic buildings and religious monuments, constantly manifests keen interest in ornament. Oftentimes artistic adornment of a building, a painting, a sculpture commissioned by a famous personage, was but one means of competing with another guild.

Perhaps this intermingling of the practical and the artistic in a unified attitude toward life is the reason posterity has seen the city of Florence as a kind of ideal city. Perhaps this is the reason one comes away from Florence feeling that the city everywhere evinces a sense of beauty and order not divorced from even the humblest aspects of life. This mixture of the abstract and the real, of the practical and the aesthetic, contributes its share to that quality called *"Fiorentinità."*

We can with some success indicate the tremendous versatility and range of the artists of the time by examining the achievement of some who dominate this age. Each of these we may say with justification lays claim to the title genius. These are Arnolfo (1237–1310?), Andrea Pisano (1270–1348), Giotto (1276–1337), and Orcagna (1308–68). Their dates span the period of our interest, and their talents represent the whole compass of Florentine art in that first great age.

Of the handful of scholars who studied with Nicola Pisano, Arnolfo, because of his contribution to Florentine civic architecture, concerns us the most. Art criticism and scholarship of the past two decades have done much to rescue Arnolfo as a sculptor from oblivion, while it has tended to deprive him somewhat of the many attributions to him as an architect. The fact remains that he is the most important artist in solid media that Florence had in the thirteenth century. The civic buildings, churches, and fortifications which are now Florence's most famous monuments are his legacy. When we stand off from the city and gaze down upon it, what catches our eye immediately is his master plan. When we recall that his name as a sculptor and former student of Nicola was already sufficiently established for him to be summoned to various cities to carry out commissions, we can with some confidence link his name with those of Dante and Giotto as one of the master spirits of Florentine culture, ushering in the greatest period of her architectural development.

The common source of our knowledge of Arnolfo is Vasari, who is unfortunately so alloyed with myth as to be unreliable. He suffers from the blindness of the present, feeling that Arnolfo's principal function was to shine as a light in the darkness for those who came after him. Modern scholarship, after almost dismissing Arnolfo, has finally resuscitated him as the great and varied artist he was.

It is possible to recognize the hand of Arnolfo in the execution of Nicola's pulpit in the Baptistry at Pisa, and we know that the magistrates of Perugia asked Charles of Anjou to allow his architect Arnolfo to assist on the fountain in Perugia. Whether he went or not, we do not know. We know that he worked with another student from Nicola's studio on the shrine of St. Dominic in the church dedicated to that saint at Bologna sometime before 1267. Here Arnolfo seemed to have been allowed considerable freedom in execution, and we recognize his hand in draperies and conformation of the figures.

His first independent works, executed in Rome, were several tomb monuments in which he superimposed a modern Gothic canopy upon the more sedate and sober style of the Roman sarcophagus, placing an effigy upon the sarcophagus and giving greater importance to the molding of the figure and the other sculptural details. This work in Rome came to rich fruition in the tomb of Cardinal de Braye at Orvieto, a work of singular beauty and balance, decorated with mosaics on the base and behind the effigy; its topmost figure is the Virgin holding the Christ child. The work as a whole is a masterpiece, and its various figures, done with majesty yet touching sorrow, evince the hand of a master influenced in the main by Roman art.

From 1285 on a variety of master works came from Arnolfo's hand: a tabernacle at St. Paul Outside the Walls in Rome; a ciborium at St. Cecilia's, also in Rome. Later toward the time of his commission for the cathedral and the Palazzo della Signoria in Florence, Pope Boniface ordered designs for his own tomb and a chapel of St. Boniface at St. Peter's. And in this period of the commissions in Florence, three pieces—a Nativity, the Dormition of the Virgin, and a Virgin and Child—exemplify the best in Arnolfo. The second of these, the Dormition, shows a recumbent draped figure of the Virgin with another figure, probably St. John, crouched at her feet. It is a tremendously moving example of medieval art. The figure of the Virgin in the Nativity, like the others, was intended to fill a lunette on the façade of the cathedral, and as such is heroic in feeling and scale. Their function on the façade of a cathedral accounts in part for the severity and massiveness of Arnolfo's figures. The Virgin, with the Child offering its benediction, holds her right hand lightly upon the shoulder of the Christ, and gazes austere and inscrutable out into the ages, an effect which is more Etruscan or Roman than Gothic. It is grave, serene, and absolutely without exuberance.

This very brief list of Arnolfo's sculpture serves to indicate that Arnolfo's characteristic manner was monumental, suggestive of a sublime reality beyond the enigmatic, impassive exteriors. Yet he was capable of borrowing an occasional flourish from the Gothic. We can see, dimly, the lines of a tradition which he is to hand on to Andrea Pisano in the spare and austere vision of the doors of the Baptistry, which in their ideality bear marked affinities with the simplifications of Arnolfo's style. Arnolfo's ideality, too, bears marked affinity with that of Giotto. The painter, from time to time, depicts architectural details which are startlingly like those of Arnolfo's designs, and his figures and the handling of drapery have a marked similarity to those of the massive forms sculpted by Arnolfo.

In the fields of architecture and civil engineering, Arnolfo was considered the best of his kind in Tuscany. To him the Florentines entrusted the construction of the third wall of the city in 1284. His reputation was established since, according to Vasari, he had designed and built in 1280 the loggia of Orsanmichele on the site of the ancient church of San Michele in Orto, to provide cover for the grain and corn market. Vasari also attributes to him the reconstruction of the principal chapel of the Badia and the restoration of the church and choir, an attribution which in our time is being vindicated by researchers. If Vasari is correct, even the bell tower—at least about a third of it—is the work of Arnolfo.

In 1294, just at the time when Dante was entering upon public life, Arnolfo was designing the great Gothic church and convent of Santa Croce for the Franciscans, including the first cloister. The church itself was, for Tuscany, a remarkable experiment in the use of space, the nave and aisles being so wide as to prevent bringing the arches under the roof. Surrendering what to some is the glory of Gothic, namely the vault, he substituted a roof of open beams. It is now recognized that the church itself has affinities with the great churches of Sicily, like the Duomo in Palermo and that in Monreale, and with some in Rome.

We have referred in the previous chapter to the building of the cathedral at which Arnolfo was at work simultaneously with Santa Croce. Built on the site of Santa Reparata, the new church was supported by funds donated by the wool guild and by taxes laid upon all exported goods, and by others levied upon the population. Like Santa Croce the design is that of the Latin Cross, with a tremendous nave, two side aisles, two transepts, and two tribunes, out of which open five chapels. The whole is surmounted by an over-whelming cupola, the work of Brunelleschi more than a century later. We assume that Arnolfo's designs were ad-hered to, since he did not live long enough to see the church completed. Scholars are still at work trying to decide from the precious remains of the original façade what kind of design the exterior bore. Since his façade was torn down in 1357 and replaced by another, the second of four, Arnolfo's work on the façade has been progressively obscured.

The people of Florence were sufficiently pleased with its progress to exempt Arnolfo in April, 1299, of all taxes, on the ground that his industry, experience, and genius were visibly producing a church which they hoped would be the most beautiful in Tuscany. The result reflects Arnolfo's eclectic handling of Gothic elements in a church which is majestic, without preciosity, demonstrating solemn purity of line free of decoration. The works of art which it con-tains remain, within this vast concept, subordinate to the whole.

Hereafter, no work of importance was undertaken with-out Arnolfo's advice. He was assigned the task of designing and building the Palazzo della Signoria, the story of which we have given in the previous chapter. The data provided by Villani are substantially repeated by Vasari, who himself examined its foundations in 1551 and found them sound. He laments that Arnolfo was not able to complete the building; but the building was sufficiently far along for Dante, with the other priors, to reside there from June 15 to August 14, 1300. It came successively under the hands of Andrea Pisano in the fourteenth century, of Michelozzo and Cronaca in the fifteenth century, and of Vasari in the sixteenth century.

We can, in looking over the achievement of Arnolfo, repeat the old judgment of Symonds: "No Italian architect has enjoyed the privilege of stamping his own individuality more strongly upon his native city than Arnolfo." If we gaze down upon the city from a near-by hill, what we see is in substance Arnolfo's plan for it. Its profile, consisting of the Duomo, the Palazzo Vecchio, Santa Croce, the Badia, Orsanmichele, the vestige of the third wall and the gates, suggests the heart and soul of Arnolfo's Florence, a persistence into time of that majestic conception with which he endowed the city.

†   †   †

Of Giotto's early life nothing is known. The tales of his birth and early youth, given us by Ghiberti and repeated by Vasari, are romantic enough to have captured the imagination of posterity and to have given them a peculiar sanction. According to this evidence, the future painter, sculptor, and architect of Florence was born about fourteen miles outside the city in the village of Vespignano. Here from 1267 on, amidst the verdant mountain meadows he tended his father's sheep, acquiring that natural sympathy for pastoral life which appears later in his painting. Gifted in design, he is supposed to have whiled away the hours drawing upon the earth with a stick or scratching upon a rock. Thus he was discovered at the age of ten by Cimabue, the great progenitor of Tuscan painting, drawing the figure of a sheep upon a smooth stone. Recognizing his talent, Cimabue arranged with the boy's father to let him be brought, under the artist's care, to Florence. "In a short time," writes Vasari, "instructed by Cimabue and aided by nature, the boy not only equalled his master in his own manner, but became so good an imitator of Nature that he totally banished the rude Greek manner, restoring art to the better path adhered to in modern times, and introducing the custom of accurately drawing living persons from life."

In the workshop of the master, the students would learn to draw and to prepare colors, grinding them under the guidance of the teacher. Cennino, in his *Libro dell' Arte,* written "in reverence of Giotto, of Taddeo and of Agnolo" sometime during the early decades of the fifteenth century, describes the practices of the painters of Giotto's own school. We may assume that these practices in fresco painting, in tempera and various kinds of drawing, stem from his own early training under the great master Cimabue.

Giotto grew up in Florence at a time when Arnolfo and Giovanni Pisano, the student son of Nicola, were great names in the world of Tuscan artistic achievement, and he saw the gradual establishment of government under the priors and the assumption of civic responsibility by the corporations of the guilds. He saw with Dante and Villani the reconstruction of old churches and the building of new ones—Santa Maria Novella, Santa Maria Maggiore, Santa Trinita all being made over in the newer Gothic mode, reflections of which were to appear in his frescoes in the Peruzzi and Bardi chapels at Santa Croce.

In 1300, the year of the Jubilee, when Giotto was thirty-three years old, along with Dante and Villani among the many who made the pilgrimage, he was in Rome, already an established artist with commissions for work in fresco and mosaic. Three frescoes were done for the Lateran Basilica, of which now only a fragment remains. For two of his commissions done slightly later, the disputed Navicella mosaic and an altarpiece for St. Peter's, he was paid enormous sums which, even if exaggerated by historians, indicate the esteem in which he was held.

Sometime between 1296 and 1304, Giotto was invited to come to Assisi where he worked on the great frescoes depicting the life of St. Francis. Here was a subject of great emotional appeal to the painter. The great saint had been the herald of a wave of spiritual enthusiasm which swept over Europe. Pure, humble, unique, St. Francis had dedicated himself to restoring the damaged house of God on the Continent. The subject which his life afforded led to a series of scenes by which his spirituality could be demonstrated and made an object of contemplation. The result has been a balance between the demands of objective reality and the higher suggestions of an ideal religiosity. We feel that, in its ideality, even if Giotto worked with assistants on the project, the motivation and the controlling purpose here are his. The training he had received at the hands of Cimabue, and his experience in Rome, where he lived for more than one period of his life, is revealed in the details of both architecture and landscape which are accurately represented. The subject matter itself seems to have been a turning point in Giotto's life, a sudden grasp of artistic form, a release into an entirely personal and native style. Whether by accident or design, the remainder of his life is tied in with other Franciscan churches and convents.

In the fourth decade of his life Giotto was at work on the frescoes for which he is best known to lovers of Florentine art: the paintings in the Peruzzi and Bardi chapels at Santa Croce, scenes from the lives of the two St. Johns, and from the life of St. Francis. Much of Giotto's work—the bulk of it, in fact—has been destroyed by whitewashing and the passage of time, but these restored paintings provide the opportunity to see Giotto's genius at its full tide. They are a remarkable advance over his days in Assisi in dramatic grasp, in the drawing and grouping of figures, in the handling of the draperies, and in the more elaborate architectural details. Here, too, we are able to feel the great warmth of personality, the tenderness, the elevation of spirit which St. Francis was able to elicit from the man. Most famous of these frescoes—perhaps deservedly so—is the scene depicting the death of Francis, a scene which had once before been executed at Assisi. Here in a vastly more simple and more affecting way is the scene which later reduced Michelangelo to tears.

It is virtually impossible to establish chronology at this point, but in this period Giotto was engaged in his other great cycle of frescoes, those in the Chapel of Our Lady in Padua. It is here that Giotto's art was perfected. In his forties, working apparently at the same time as Giovanni Pisano whose marble Madonna stood over the entrance, Giotto's reputation was at its zenith. His task was to cover the walls and ceilings of the plain rectangular chapel with fresco decoration. The ceiling he painted simply, in blue, with medallions containing depictions of Christ, the Virgin, and eight prophets divided equally into two broad fields. The entrance wall shows the Last Judgment; above the arch, God the Father with angels on either side; above the apsidal arch, the scene of the Annunciation; along the walls, three rows of scenes, thirty-four in all, from the lives of the Virgin and Christ, with Joachim and Anna. The lower sections of the walls depict the vices and virtues. It would seem that there is here a better grasp of perspective in the handling of volume and space; we may note the confidence of placing buildings on angles, and the successful attempts at rendering depth, of grouping figures in various degrees of light. Although Giotto's paintings have undergone restoration almost to the point of destroying the possibility of our seeing perfectly what he intended, still the pictures convey an atmosphere which is absent in the other cycle at Assisi.

The landscapes, like the architectural details, are only as naturalistic as serves the need of the painting; that is, they are a support for the symbolic sense to be conveyed, the poetry to be suggested. For example, in the flight into Egypt, the mountains and trees are tangible and solid, but wanting in a proportional relation to the figures. What is conveyed is the seriousness of a stern and sad Virgin, somewhat preoccupied as if with the fate of her child. All the figures, including that of the ass, are in the position of movement toward the right, and even the angel who watches above has his right arm pointed out of the picture. In another, the mourning over Christ's body, the naked Christ is surrounded by mourners in expressive attitudes. Overhead there are angels in expressions of great grief. The landscape itself corresponds with the desolation of sorrow by being rendered bare and snowy.

In the closing years of his life Giotto is difficult to track down. In 1313 he was in Rome, for what reason we do not know. His name becomes associated with Rimini, Avignon, Lucca, Arezzo, and even Paris, according to Vasari. In the

late 1320's, after completing a charge for Charles of Calabria, then governor of Florence, Giotto was summoned to
Naples by Charles' father, King Robert, for the purpose of
executing certain paintings in the royal residence and elsewhere. These unfortunately are all lost. They might have
given us some idea of Giotto's manner in his advanced years.

This commission is one proof among many of Giotto's
great renown. The peasant boy who became the famous
painter is received into a king's household as one of the
family with donations for expenses incurred in his work.
As always, it is likely that he had under his tutelage workers
and apprentices to carry out his designs. From this period
comes the humorous tale of a verbal exchange, one of several preserved by such writers as Boccaccio and Sacchetti,
and repeated by Vasari. "Well, Giotto," the king said one
summer day, "if I were you, I would stop painting when
the weather is so hot." To which Giotto wryly commented,
"So would I, if I were King Robert."

Stories about Giotto all reveal a sharp, sardonic, somewhat caustic wit at variance with the character of the artist
that we sentimentalize out of his paintings. The quality
they demonstrate is typically hardheaded, Italian.

Much of medieval wit has a note of pungency, especially
in the rising realism of the time. Giotto was Italian to the
core, practical about money matters, on more than one
occasion going to court for establishing settlements. A
satirical bent which we note in these tales he himself cor-
roborates in the song against voluntary poverty which bears
his name. Since he was perhaps the highest paid artist in
Italy, rich in money and lands, there is an irony that his
poem should honestly express his own aversion to being
poor and at the same time that his reputation depends

largely upon the depiction of poverty in the person of St. Francis. Like Dante he recognized that hypocrisy could disguise itself in clerical garb, and his honesty with regard to finance, and his reverence for a fruitful, gainful existence, while self-defensive, is a mark of his independent spirit.

Honored throughout Europe, wealthy, blessed in children, the originator of a school of painting whose students would perpetuate his name well on into the next century, Giotto received the final accolade: he was named headmaster of the cathedral, of the civic walls and fortifications. Although we are prepared by no data for Giotto's qualifications in this field, a document names him in 1334 as the best qualified for the job. Out of these remaining three years of his life came the design for and bottom sections of the wonderful bell tower which is a landmark in Florence today.

The sculptured reliefs which circle the base in two rows have always been ascribed to Giotto, at least in design and partially in execution. Ghiberti the sculptor (1378–1455) could say later in his commentary that he had himself seen "preparatory designs" by Giotto's hand for these reliefs, most excellently designed. The new emergence into fame as sculptor and architect is like his youthful renown as a mosaicist, a factor which we cannot account for except on the grounds of his environment and his genius.

The universal geniuses, like Orcagna shortly after Giotto's time, were trained in a variety of disciplines. We may remember, too, that the Florence into which Giotto came was already under the sway of the great Arnolfo, whom he may have known, and with whom he may even have been in Rome. Scholars have come to see reflections of Arnolfo in Giotto's paintings, not only in architectural details but in the modeling of figures and of draperies, and in the general control of volume. It is peculiarly fitting that, after a long lag in the work on the Duomo, Giotto should take up Arnolfo's masterpiece and provide for that monument of his, a companion to it.

Within months the cornerstone was laid, and in the next three years, the two lower stories were completed with some of the decorative reliefs. Giotto's companion in the sculptures was Andrea Pisano, his successor as master-builder for Florence. Florence itself, perhaps mindful of an obligation to the great artists who belonged to her and recollecting the harsh and unjust treatment of Dante, had gathered to herself the greatest artist of the day, and went so far as to state that the appointment as *capomaestro* was made partly to insure that he would live in Florence, "for by his presence many can have the advantage of his wisdom and learning, and the city shall gain no small honor because of him." After a short visit to Milano, according to Villani, where Florence, for political reasons, had sent the old man, possibly to perform some art work for the Visconti, Giotto died on January 8, 1337.

Dante we recall, in speaking of fickle fame, names Giotto as the painter who had surpassed the reputation of Cimabue. Both Petrarch and Boccaccio speak highly—even affectionately—of him as a person and as an innovator in art. Pucci the contemporary poet, Giovanni Villani the historian, Sacchetti the writer of tales, and even Cristoforo Landino in his commentary on the *Divine Comedy*, praise him as a leader and initiator. All attest to a genius of the first rank. Lorenzo the Magnificent, after one hundred years, had Politian comprise a suitable epitaph. Let it stand here as the testament of the ages: "Lo, I am he by whom dead painting was restored to life, to whose right hand all was possible, by whom art became one with nature. No one ever painted more or better. Do you wonder at yon fair tower which holds the sacred bells? Know that it was I who bade her first rise towards the stars. For I am Giotto— what need is there to tell of my work? Long as verse lives, my name shall endure!" (Translated by Julia Cartwright.)

† † †

Of Andrea Pisano da Pontedera's youth not much is known, but old reports have it that he had acquired his early training in Pisa, probably as a student of Giovanni, son of Nicola, and had spent some time in Venice during which he had carved several pieces for the façade of St. Mark's. Very early he seems to have acquired a reputation as both an architect and a bronze caster, as well as a sculptor. We first hear of him in Florence for the commission of the first bronze doors of the Baptistry.

The project to supply bronze doors for the Baptistry was initiated at least as early at 1322 by the Opera di San Giovanni, perhaps with the idea of inviting Tino di Camaino to work on the designs. The first idea entertained was that the doors would be of wood covered with gilded metal (*"di rame dorato o di metallo"*) as was the common practice. But a look at the glorious doors on the cathedral at Pisa seems to have persuaded otherwise. In 1329 once again the decision for bronze doors was affirmed. Piero di Jacopo was sent to Pisa to make drawings of the Pisa doors, and thence to Venice to search for a master of the project. Out of the search came the commission for Andrea, and from the spotty records we can piece together the various stages in the making of the doors: the building of the wooden

77

frames or models, the modeling of the designs in wax, the casting of the doors, and finally the employment of the gold-smith for the gilding of the doors from 1332 to 1335. After remedying certain flaws in the casting, Andrea mounted the doors in 1336. Of this occasion Giovanni Villani writes with pride: "These doors are beautiful in the extreme, of exceptional workmanship, and costly . . . I, the author, speaking for the Calimala Merchants' Gild, financial sup-porters of the Opera di San Giovanni, was the officer com-missioning this work." The inscription on the door bears the name of the designer-sculptor, and that of his son Nino, who served as his assistant.

The plan for each of the two doors was the depiction of fourteen rectangular reliefs on each door set in pairs. Each relief was to be executed and cast separately; then the figures were to be gilded, leaving the background a natural bronze. Each relief was then to be set into the larger frame. The frame itself, at the corners of each relief, was to con-tain small gilded lions' heads, twenty-four in number for each door. These replaced the customary rosettes with a symbol dear to the Florentine heart. The four lowest reliefs on each door depict single figures of the Virtues; the ten upper reliefs on each door represent with more complexity scenes from the life of John the Baptist, ranging from his birth to his burial. Each scene is enclosed by a frame in the form of a quadrilobe medallion, a French Gothic influence which affords considerable contrast to the lineal severity of the visual ordering of the panels. The whole effect is one of great elegance and line containing the individual scenes. Some of the scenes seem clearly derived from mo-saics within the Baptistry, thus affording a unifying factor with the art within.

It is difficult to do justice to Andrea's work on the doors. The sentiments are strongly influenced by Giotto. Vasari points out that it was Giotto's work actually that freed Andrea from a certain coarseness. Whether this is true or not, upon his native skill as a metal worker and sculptor Andrea imposed a simplicity and purity of design, a true elegance in the handling of draperies, and a tender and affecting spirituality which link him to the master. Their common spirit, their tendency to create massive rather than delicate figures, their intellectual as well as spiritual affinity make their association not only more likely but in actuality more successful. When in 1334, Giotto became the chief architect of the cathedral and worked on the campanile, he supervised the lower section of the tower and its decorative elements, and, according to tradition, employed Andrea's talents as sculptor and co-worker in the execution of the two rows of reliefs.

Some of these may actually have been carved by Giotto, as Antonio Pucci, in 1373, opined in his *Centiloquio*, and as Ghiberti reiterates in his famous *Commentaries*. The greatest number of reliefs of the lower row have been attributed, however, to Andrea, although it is entirely possible, as Vasari repeatedly suggests, that Giotto provided the designs from which Andrea worked. If we assume that the work on the reliefs was begun at the time the campanile was being built, and assume further the friendship of these two artists, this degree of collaboration is not unusual.

Upon Giotto's death, Andrea succeeded him as *capo-maèstro* of the cathedral works and continued the work on the campanile. It is likely that the greater part of the reliefs were done during his tour of duty. During this time he modified Giotto's plan to include on a level above the reliefs four niches on each face of the structure, each to contain a statue. Eight of these were soon completed, including sibyls, prophets, and Solomon and David, parts of which Andrea himself seems to have executed, and for which he must have provided the designs. These figures are now in the Museum of the Opera del Duomo.

In 1343, Andrea departed from Florence to go to Pisa and ultimately to Orvieto where he became *campomaestro,* and where he died in 1349. While we associate his name almost entirely with the bronze doors of the Baptistry and with the reliefs on the campanile, Vasari reminds us that Walter de Brienne, duke of Athens, hired Andrea to strengthen his security in the Signoria by placing iron grating on all the windows of the first floor, erecting an additional wall leading from the palace containing a secret stairway, and also putting up a great door. (The door subsequently was destroyed in the Florentine attempt to efface the memory of the despot.) The purpose of the despot was obviously to make the *palazzo* into a fortress, even if it meant appropriating work from the Ponte Vecchio "without any consideration for the public convenience."

During his lifetime, Andrea influenced many students and left as a legacy his sculptor and architect son, Nino, and his greatest student, the renowned Andrea Orcagna.

The last genius of the age whom we shall discuss is Andrea di Cione, called Orcagna, hailed by Vasari as painter, architect, sculptor, and poet. To this we should have to add goldsmith and mosaicist, as the glorious tabernacle in Orsanmichele makes clear. Schooled by Andrea Pisano, he appears in a variety of documents between 1343 and 1368. Once we find him enrolled in the guild of doctors and apothecaries; on another occasion his name appears third on a list of the five most renowned artists of Florence, from whom one was to be chosen to do an altarpiece for a church in Pistoia. In 1352 and 1354 he was given a commission to paint an altarpiece. This commission is the famous masterpiece for the altar of the Strozzi Chapel in Santa Maria Novella, the only authenticated work in this medium which he signed, dated 1357. In 1352 he became a member of the guild of sculptors and stonemasons, and in the next few years his name appears as sponsor for artists coming into the guild. From this time on his fame increases and we find him as *capomaèstro* of Orsanmichele in 1355. From this period stemmed the tabernacle which occupied his energy for some years in its design and execution.

Other occupations filled his time and talents: the preparation of plans for changes in the Duomo, the acceptance of the job of *campomaestro* for the cathedral at Orvieto, and the work to carry on simultaneously in both cities. With his brother Matthew he supervised the mosaics on the façade at Orvieto, and the completion of the tabernacle in Florence. Forced to give up his commission in Orvieto by the Orvietans who wanted his services full time, he finally finished a mosaic there in 1361. In the next year he was again occupied with the Florentine cathedral. One of his assignments, an altarpiece of St. Matthew for the Arte del Cambio, was completed by his brother Jacob on account of Andrea's illness. This is the year 1368, after which the records are nonexistent.

Andrea's prowess as a sculptor is represented by his tabernacle, as his skill as a painter is evinced by the Strozzi masterpiece; each in its way is perhaps the most distinguished art object of the time. He is sufficiently talented to rank as the first of the universal artists in Florence culminating in Michelangelo and Leonardo da Vinci.

Many of the artists of the second half of the century felt themselves to be followers of the earlier masters. But Florence itself had passed through a series of crises which affect art: famine and bank failures, the despotism of the Duke of Athens, the horrors of the Black Death in the middle of the century, and in the years immediately following, wars and civil strife. Orcagna came out of this period, and the paintings which he subsequently executed with his brother Nardo in Santa Maria Novella, under the influence of Dante, reflect the somberness and severity of the age. If we restrict ourselves only to the authentic paintings, we see something of a profound detachment, of an ideality which comes through the dark, deep-set eyes of his figures, looking out upon our world with something like admonition in their glance.

It was a time of great somberness. Giovanni Villani rehearses the details of the Plague, and Boccaccio who remembered it well gives us ample proof as well as details of the dissolution and horror of a time which in Florence carried off almost one hundred thousand people within a period of a few weeks. Orcagna and his friends, who had seen the death of their teacher and fellow artists, chose the way of an increased religious dedication and sublimated the horror of the time by depicting it in their work, like the fragment of the Triumph of Death in Santa Croce showing cripples and beggars asking Death to take them. Ironically Death in these fragments chooses the strong and the healthy. These murals, unfortunately destroyed, are lost to us as one of the most valuable commentaries upon the

Plague of 1348. Beside the fragment, two others depict a cardinal and some women, dead, and some falling houses with people escaping through the door of one of them. These afford a wonderful example of Orcagna's ability to depict the grimmer details of life in an almost unparalleled example of medieval realism. These fragments Ghiberti, in his commentaries, calls "three magnificent tales from the hand of that most noble master."

In this same passage Ghiberti praises Orcagna for being equally adept at sculpture and painting. Orcagna himself liked to sign his paintings "sculptor," and his sculptures "pictor." According to Vasari, he did so "so that men should be aware of his claims as a sculptor while they were admiring his paintings, and of his talents as a painter while they were examining his sculptures." We have no doubt concerning his skill when we examine first the tabernacle of Orsanmichele and then the Strozzi masterpiece.

We may piece together the story of the tabernacle from Ghiberti and Vasari. The brotherhood of Orsanmichele, after the ravages of the Black Death, had become very wealthy in donations made to the Madonna. It is a curiosity of the time, recounted by the contemporary historians, that wealth could not be displayed in dress and other adornments. As a consequence money was lavished upon public building. The fear of death during the Plague had elicited many promises, which upon fulfillment swelled the coffers of the various religious organizations. Orcagna was commissioned to provide a fitting shrine or tabernacle for the Madonna portrait painted by Daddi in 1346. The work on the tabernacle was started in the fifties.

The tabernacle, in its completed form, whether seen from front or back, dazzles the mind and eye. Since it combines marbles, mosaic, enamels, gilded glass, *pietra dura,* bas-reliefs, intaglios, and statuettes, sufficient to elicit a poem of praise from Sacchetti, we must content ourselves with a brief description of it.

The front is an altar over which is the picture of the Madonna and Child. Above this is the open roof with crowning statuettes of the Archangel Michael and an angel. Around the base on the front and the sides there are reliefs in octagonal recesses presenting scenes from the life of the Virgin: her birth, presentation, and marriage, the Annunciation, Nativity, adoration of the Magi, the Presentation of Christ in the Temple, and finally a scene showing the aged Mary receiving word of her own approaching death.

The back of the tabernacle is entirely made up of sculptures, a great relief showing the death and Assumption of the Virgin, a feat stupendous in the history of Tuscan sculpture, which covers the entire height of the tabernacle. The bottom section shows the Madonna lying upon a couch with the apostles around her. Among them, according to Ghiberti, is Orcagna himself with a hood and small beard, and above is depicted the miraculous Ascension in the *mandorla;* Mary is surrounded by six angels, and she is depicted in the action of dropping her girdle to the astonished St. Thomas.

The sentiment expressed by this miracle of the arts has been expressed beautifully by W. R. Valentier: "The artist, inclined to a pessimistic conception of life, could here express with all the psychological power at his command, the ordeal and suffering through which the people of the city and he himself had passed. The sorrow of the apostles standing by the dying Virgin is not conveyed by extravagant gestures but with restrained though nonetheless convincing and affecting attitudes. They do not throw their arms into the air, as we see in earlier representations, but press their wringing hands towards their mouths, hold their cheeks with both hands or lift their arms slightly in front of their breasts with gestures of horrified astonishment. The faces with the half-opened, crying mouths and the eyes closed and blinded with too much weeping, are embodiments of deep despair. The mass of spectators pressed close together behind the death bed with its wide expanse of white linen, seems like soaring waves of an ocean filled with endless mourning before an empty beach. ("Orcagna and the Black Death of 1348," *Art Quarterly,* Vol. XII [1949], 116.)

In the emotions which are allowed to show here, and in the depiction of the Madonna, we see a deepening of the spirit that the age elicited from the artist, causing in his work a reaction against the sweetness and excessive lyricisms of, say, Nino or Giovanni Pisano. The Madonna shows the effects of suffering; her face is stern, her eyes are deep set, and in her life and in that of the apostles around her, Orcagna, through a sublimated realism, restores to art its essential subject matter and its profounder sentiments.

The Strozzi altarpiece in Santa Maria Novella depicts, in a central panel or compartment out of five, Christ enthroned with worshiping angels. To the right the Virgin presents St. Thomas Aquinas; on the left John the Baptist introduces St. Peter; St. Thomas is receiving the Gospels and St. Peter the keys from the Christ. St. Catherine and St. Michael are behind the Virgin at one end, and St. Paul and St. Lawrence are at the opposite end. The whole design is austere and symmetrical. The Christ is connected by symmetrical lines to the other figures, giving a monumental, grand, and severe effect. The severity is mitigated somehow by the range of color: azure, carmine, orange, amethyst, blue, gray, black, and gold. Much that suggests the textiles of the Middle Ages is to be seen in the actual textures; Catherine's brocade, for example, has an interesting pattern of palmetto leaves and buds. The handling of the draperies is especially persuasive, particularly in the figure of St. Paul. In the skill in the draperies perhaps we are seeing a carry-over from the skill achieved in his sculptures, but in their technique Orcagna looks forward to the next great age of painting.

4. House and Home

FLORENTINE SOCIAL STRUCTURE in the twelfth century was dominated by the aristocracy, and the subsequent century saw the gradual merging of this class with that of the prosperous merchants to form the upper stratum. With the enrichment of this upper level of society and the growing pride of city which accompanied the distribution of power among the major guilds, architecture became an expression, both civic and private, of the new prosperity.

The tower stronghold of the nobles seems to have been the basic building unit not only of Florence but of the hill cities of Tuscany and Umbria: a base ten to fifteen feet on a side, the size of a single room, and on it room upon room raised up successively. The model is not different from the form which came quite naturally to Giotto when he constructed the first stories of his famous bell tower. With a rising crush of population between the successive walls of ancient Florence, such a construction would offer multiple advantages by conserving valuable space and providing safety from enemies.

Attempts to adorn the severe exterior as well as increase the graces of living provided gradually for beam-and-strut-supported balconies with roofs. These provided air and light for the inhabitants; at a top story, they were a means of offense in times of strife. With the upward thrust of building necessitated by the growing population, bracket supports of stone and brick for galleries began to define the outer form of Florentine building. When in 1250 the towers were drastically reduced in height, the need for living space brought about an ingenious solution. Unable to build upward, or to encroach upon the already-jammed narrow streets, Florentine builders made the balconies or galleries permanent from the first story up, constructing them of brick or timber and running the new façade up to the roof line. Serving a practical purpose, they became so popular an addition to Florentine houses as to cause one section of the Via Tornabuoni to be called the Street of the Beautiful Galleries (La Via dei Belli Sporti). Gradually victimized by taxes (7,000 gold florins a year) and restricted by law, they reached their end, in 1533, in the decree of Alexander de' Medici, who ordered them destroyed or removed. Never completely eliminated, survivals continued to establish a mode which is still being imitated in modern construction.

From these galleries in the earlier periods, before the more permanent *sporti*, on days of celebration, to welcome visitors or to enjoy a *festa,* the inhabitants would hang out their tapestries and banners, a welcome change from the usual gray severity of the day-to-day structure. Later, on the fronts of the buildings there would be other means of supporting the gay hangings, perhaps a single bar extending across the windows about midway between top and bottom. Hooks and rings at the sides of windows would be used for airing birds in their cages, or for dogs or pet monkeys let out onto the gallery for light and air. There would be, too, torch sockets, ornate lanterns of wrought iron, great rings and hooks low on the walls for making fast beasts of burden.

Before the birth of Dante these buildings presented, on

the outskirts of the walls, a stalwart line, keeping most of their window space on the street side, and forming on both sides of the street what is called a *borgo*. Inside the walls, however, the square formation of the ancient city, with streets running north-south and east-west, produced rectangular building areas. These, occupied by families or clans of up to forty or fifty people, resulted in building complexes related to each other architecturally as well as socially, sharing a common piazza, well, and church. Subject to the inevitable changes resulting from defections in family alliances, death, sale of property, and new lanes between building sites, the face of the city gradually changed. To overcome the difficulties afforded by the new streets, archways spanned the streets to preserve the connection between the buildings. By means of these, the inhabitants could, even in time of street wars, maintain contact with other members of their groups. These too, like the galleries, were severely taxed.

When in 1250 the heights of towers came down to fifty *braccia*, the result was a group of joined buildings around a court, giving an appearance of some uniformity by the retention of a stone gallery at the top. Thus joined together, they became, with their central court, the *palazzo* of the late thirteenth and early fourteenth centuries.

The ground floor, securely separated from the upper stories, was let out to various venders or artisans or used by the merchant for his own affairs. When the tower house occupied a corner, the ground floor might become a loggia for family pleasure or for business. Encroaching on the street and provided with roof and pillars, as in the still-existing loggia of the Alberti on the Via dei Benci, the loggia provided a model for more ambitious structures. In and just beyond Dante's time, as structures even apart from family dwellings they appear in historical records, signs of the wealth of their builders, meeting places for family and friends. In time the loggia assumed civic importance, with its grandest manifestations in the impressive Loggia dei Lanzi, in the beautiful Orsanmichele, the converted grain market, and in the New Market—an amazing transformation of a basement room, but retaining its characteristics—vaults, arches, roofs, but open to the street.

The roof line, too, began to take on the appearance familiar today. As the *sporti* became a welcome part of fourteenth-century structure, they tended to hide the battlemented crowns. To provide cover, now the roof itself, slanted slightly downward, overhung the *sporti*. The *sporti* themselves overhung the street, thus producing till this day the appearance of narrow distances between houses on either side of the street. Below the roof, for air and sun, there came into existence the top-floor *terrazza* or loggia which the Renascence was to refine with columns and pillars in its imitation of antiquity. Below, on the street, sheltered from rain by the successive projections of *sporti* and roof, along the front of the *palazzo* appeared the stone bench running the length of the building, a resting place for whiling away summer evenings in pleasant chatter.

† † †

Villani tells us that people came from afar to see and admire the beautiful *palazzi* of Florence. Over the course of 150 years, great changes had been taking place in living conditions as a result of the great growth of commerce and industry. Money, in providing more of the graces of living, also drew from pulpit and poet alike disapproval of the new luxury. For Dante the present may have seemed a terrible degeneration from the sober past, but the perspective of history enables us to see from his own time forward a burst of artistic and spiritual energy which is precisely the fruit of the new riches. Money vaunted the selfish as well as un-selfish interests of its owners, as it has always done. Life became more luxurious for some, but for many it merely became more bearable.

If we look at one of the houses, what shall we see? Above the door, itself impressive in its bars and bolts, the family arms, the mark of status and prestige; across the façade, flanking the main door, windows protected by iron bars or grillwork. The windows above, narrow and small, would be covered by cloth, linen or cotton, which had been oiled and mounted in frames. Later these would be painted with geometric designs as part of the decoration. As we see in paintings of the time, these were hinged so that the bottom half could be pushed out and fixed for ventilation; they could also be raised like the modern blind. Glass itself was a very great luxury, and made only rare appearances in the richest houses in isolated decorative windows. So luxurious were they deemed to be that Blessed Simone Fidati offered the view that the use of glass had, among other graver causes, provoked God's wrath and brought on the great flood of 1333.

Within, in an ideal house, we would find a small court where the well was located, along with the first-floor stor-age. From the court would rise the stairway, leading upward to the living quarters. In commoner houses lacking courts the staircase would be placed in full view on the outer wall, perhaps entering at the first upper level and connecting with the other floors within. The courtyard and any downstairs rooms would more than likely be paved with brick. A luxurious addition on this ground floor would be a paved loggia, used for entertaining, and painted with bright frescoes in keeping with the financial standing of the owner. It would be, further, ideally suited by its position for the brighter aspects of living, like music and dancing, to which even the casual passer-by would be attracted. This loggia would serve a quite different function from the top-floor terrace where rugs and blankets could be aired or clothes dried, and where the family could catch the breeze off the surrounding hills of an evening. Here too, according to Sacchetti, the ladies tried desperately to bleach their hair by long exposure to the sun.

The upstairs rooms included the *sala madornale* (the principal living room), the kitchen, and the bedrooms. The location of the kitchen would perforce be high in the house to provide for the escape of smoke from the cooking fires. Until the wider use of chimneys, the kitchen thus gravitated either upward or out of the house proper. The fear of fire was a natural one for the age, even when houses were constructed mainly of brick and stone, inasmuch as fire was the weapon of destruction in party strife. On more than one occasion Villani writes of wholesale destruction of parts of the city owing to the incendiaries of the time. Boccaccio's friend Paolo da Certaldo advises householders to keep ready a rope "long enough to reach from roof to ground, so as to enable you to escape from the window."

Kitchen equipment included a wooden dining table, a wooden sink, and various containers for salt, for sugar, and for flour. There would be a variety of cooking utensils, and iron, brass, or copper vessels. Even in the houses of the rich, there were not great numbers of plates and cutlery.

Forks and spoons, plates and bowls were coming more and more into use, although in Dante's time, two priors at a table shared a single dish.

The living room might contain, among its luxuries, a fireplace with its chimney enclosed in the walls, an improvement over open fires in earthenware boxes placed in the middle of a room with no provision for venting smoke. There would also be a long narrow table, probably on trestles or "horses," other round, multiple-use tables, and some chairs and benches. The walls might be bare, but high on the wall there would be a series of hooks from which to suspend wall coverings of various rich stuffs. These served as an insulation against the cold as well as decoration. As the age wore on, the hangings were supplanted by designs actually painted on the wall in imitation of the rich tapestries. Above them appeared highly decorative borders of fruit and flowers or birds. For festive occasions special hangings were employed, to be returned to their chests when the feast day had passed. Such holidays, with the decoration of the inside as well as the outside of the house with bright colors suspended from windows, afforded one occasion to thrust aside for the moment a habitual Tuscan sense of economy.

In the bedroom, behind the bed, perhaps in its origins a protection against the cold, was the *capoletto,* soon transformed into an embellishment for other walls as well. For practical purposes, there were also a canopy and curtains against the cold. Mattresses and warm stuffed coverlets with additional wool blankets were essential since bed clothes were apparently not used, the inhabitants sleeping naked.

By far the most widely used items of furniture were chests and cases or coffers, often highly decorative and brightly painted, used not only in the bedroom but elsewhere as well. Essential storage units, they might be large enough to form the base of a bed, or small enough to serve as jewelry and trinket boxes. In general their use is the obvious one of serving to store linens, draperies, vestments of all sorts; they might also serve as additional seating.

Alberti, in his "Del Governo della Famiglia," describes a scene of the late fourteenth century in which a husband leads his new bride into the bedchamber to show her the precious silver, tapestries, precious stones, all locked away in chests and coffers. Another chest, containing his papers, is locked up in his study, "into which place I never gave my wife permission to enter." The most usual items stored in the chests were, naturally, the linens. The inventory of Margherita, the wife of the wealthy Francesco Datini, merchant of Prato and Florence, included a surprising array of table and bed linens, napkins, various towels, and table-cloths.

Floor covering appears in paintings of the period, although the general term *tappeto* may mean virtually any kind of cover thrown over the foot of the bed, or lying at the side of it to insulate the feet of a newly risen sleeper against the cold. It would constitute one practical yet decorative item in the bedroom, like the *capoletto*. In the bedroom too we see pious paintings dealing with sacred subjects, beautiful in themselves yet serving like the frescoes on the walls of Florentine churches as objects of contemplation. The range of subjects is familiar: a Virgin with the Christ child, or a picture of St. Anne, especially dear to Florentines since 1343 when the tyrant Duke of Athens was driven from the city on her feast day, or a scene from the life of the Baptist or the Christ, as a means of stirring the heart to piety.

Among the decorations we must mention too the ornamented cradle, and, as a gift to the new mother, the *desco da parto* or "birthing tray," a richly painted and highly decorative embellishment for the bedroom.

5. Within the Family Circle

The Parent

FROM ANCIENT ROMAN DAYS and through the Langobard domination, the family was a sacred institution. The father controlled the liberty of his wife and children, and all goods. Successive generations of grandchildren within his lifetime were also subject to his jurisdiction. When a woman passed from the control of her father through marriage, she merely entered that of her husband in a virtually indissoluble tie. Her influence was that of the *domina* within the sanctuary of her house, guarding the domestic hearth, caring for objects sacred to family, watching over her children's education, assisting her husband in management of their common patrimony.

The family was the fundamental unit of society, a source of strength and security amidst the turbulent and often violent affairs of the day. Male-dominated, its strength lay in numbers as well as in capital, since it was a political as well as an economic and social center. Alberti, writing in the first half of the fifteenth century, describes in a father's terms a sense of "clan," which obtained as much for the fourteenth century as for his own time: "Quite different is the regard one has from his own family from that which he has from others, citizens or strangers, quite different the respect, authority, and reputation of the man who is backed by his family; he is more feared, more esteemed than the man with few supporters of his own. And so much more recognized and highly regarded will be the father of a family when it is large than when he is alone."

It is clear that the family afforded security, providing man power as well as financial security. Its numbers are astounding by modern standards; it included not merely wives and children, legitimate and otherwise, but servants, a husband's sisters, an aunt or an uncle, a few cousins and their children, and even, in the families of merchants, some of the employees. The head of the family felt a responsibility to the family as an entity, and to it he owed his first obligation, controlling its capital and increasing it as a sacred obligation. It is an ancient attitude toward money and property which we see so often in Dante, an insistence that property and money, in their use, are a reflection of the very personality of the creature, and a holy charge.

The father's authority over his children was absolute; his responsibility was to the family as a group. A daughter would leave for marriage, taking her dowry with her, but a son would bring his wife home. On occasion her children would be reared along with various natural children of the family, not uncommon in the age. The rearing of all the children was apt to be strict. A sonnet of Antonio Pucci offers some insight into parent-child relations. A foolish child requires the birch and a scolding word; past seven, he needs the correction of force; past fifteen, the stick; if folly persists past the age of twenty, he is to be confined and kept on short rations; past thirty, he is to be deemed incorrigible and disowned, however painful this may be to a parent.

The Education of Girls

A girl is destined for either marriage or the nunnery, and

97

so her training differs vastly from that of a boy. Since fat was thought to be the fomenter of sloth and sensuality, she was to be fed only sparingly. She was to be taught to read only if she were destined for the religious life. Alberti writes that nothing seems so essential to family life as respectful, obedient children, and this applies as much to girls as to boys. He is perfectly in accord with his earlier contemporary Ser Paolo da Certaldo, who finds woman lightsome and unstable, a "weak creature in peril of temptation as long as she is without a husband." A girl was to be given a close home training, kept busy at a variety of household chores. She should be taught to bake bread, cook poultry, wash clothes, make beds, sew, embroider, and repair hose and the like, so that when she was married, it would not be said of her that she was reared in the wilds, and her father would be praised for her upbringing. Such a course of study for a young lady would be impressed upon her early, since from the ages of twelve to fourteen, her marriage would be imminent.

Paolo's suggestion that it is not good for a young lady destined for marriage to read finds an echo in Alberti's horror of having a wife know anything of his written records. "My books and my writings," he has his character say, "I kept secret and locked up, so that she could never either read or even see them." Some women did, however, learn to read. Francesco Datini's illegitimate daughter Ginevra was taught to read, and his wife, Margherita, when she was past thirty, was taught by her husband's good friend Lapo Mazzei. He wrote to her husband in 1396: "Tell Monna Margherita that I will not write her at all unless she writes a little something to me. I want to know how good she is at writing."

In the company of a nurse or her mother, a young lady could go out—to church. The ideal held before her was that of the Virgin Mary, and it was not unusual for the pictures of a child's bedroom to feature a scene like the Annunciation. Virginity was a wistful hope, if we may trust the preaching of the time, and we recall Boccaccio's assertion that a mouth, oft-kissed, does not lose its bloom.

Some women did not wish to marry at all, and actually preferred the life of the nunnery. Two pathetic sonnets of a young lady, called the "Compiuta Donzella," sing sadly of a compulsory marriage. For her, and for many, marriage was their destiny, arranged for whatever reason by the father.

On this score, Paolo da Certaldo advises knowing something of the parents and grandparents, since it is always possible that a daughter of a good mother may inherit a bad trait from the previous generation. One must be careful of marrying into a family in which there is consumption, scrofula, madness, scurvy, or gout, for the sake of future children. One must be assured both of physical beauty and of moral virtue in a wife so that one's children may be good ones. Paolo warns against marrying a widow; she will make comparisons between the living and the dead. And if it is one's misfortune to marry more than once, he advises, marry a woman not better born than the first so that she may never insist upon advantages which were denied to the first wife.

Marriages, once planned, were arranged in a series of careful maneuvers. A young man might jog his father's mind about a young lady, but the arrangements would usually be made independent of the son's wishes. It would be more likely for the father of a young girl to pick the kind of son he would like for his daughter, one who was not only of good family and had prospects, but who also had begun to show signs of maturity and dependability. When the parents of both boy and girl were satisfied as to all the requirements and had fully discussed the terms on which the marriage would be effected, a ceremony was held without the presence of the future bride: having decided on the dowry, the male members of the two families shook hands before witnesses. Although this little ceremony might take place in a church or on its porch, the officiating member was a notary, not a priest, whose function it was to draw up the contract and record the signatures of its parties. Theoretically the number of guests who witnessed the handshake was restricted, but in practice, any interested persons could attend.

The second stage was the betrothal. Here the bride was presented to the bridegroom by her father, and the bridegroom gave the girl his ring. This took place, like the five marriages of Chaucer's Wife of Bath, at the church door. Here was offered the opportunity for anyone to raise objections to the marriage, and the father himself might offer his guarantees that his daughter did not oppose the union. This part of the arrangement was of the greatest importance and could not be broken, as we recall that the breaking of a betrothal brought about the murder of Buondelmonte and pitched Florence into one hundred years of internal dissension.

The husband-to-be, having matched the dowry with a gift of his own, could look forward to the marriage itself after a lapse of at least two weeks. Oftentimes the date of the marriage could not be set owing to the excessive youth of the bride; notarial data from the time insist on an outside time limit of ten years. We can see something of the importance of the betrothal ceremony even this far ahead of the marital union when we consider that it might serve to lessen the political friction between warring families.

For older children, marriage followed close upon the betrothal, the age of twelve being considered, since Langobardian days, the minimum age permitted. Dante and Gemma, we recall, were betrothed before they were twelve. In all of this it will be noted that the essential element was the consent of the young couple and the bond suggested by the bestowing of the ring. Both in theory and in fact, unions were affected by the exchange of a ring, as Boccaccio records, "only in the presence of God." And in some cases the ring had pledged two persons long before the contracting stage had been attained.

Banquets feted every stage of the marriage arrangements. First, a *convivium* for the two families upon completion of the contract, then another at the betrothal, and another, later, when the bride returned after a few days of marriage to her father's house for a brief period.

Sumptuary laws over the course of a century restricted all phases of life, including the wedding celebrations, which increased in splendor as wealth increased. The records of the fourteenth century are replete with descriptions of sumptuous celebrations attended by what seem to be hordes of persons, processions which include a company of knights, heralds, and trumpeters, for the nobility or the rich merchants. The banquets themselves were splendid affairs for which there were specially hired caterers, cooks, and extra servants; and the food, restricted to three courses, yet could miraculously include roasts, various poultries, fish, and a variety of meat pies.

In spite of Dante's and Villani's insistence upon the conservatism of the former age, the range of the dowry brought by the bride to marriage far exceeded the chroniclers' figure of 200 lire as a normal sum. Even taking into account the difference in the value of money, the dowries of the daughters of the new rich were extravagantly high and threw a certain cast of irony over Gemma's poor dowry of 200 lire, when she married Dante. These dowries, added to the cost of the expensive trousseau and linens and of banquets, make us recall Dante's remark that in his time many a father dreaded the birth of girls. Nonetheless, marriage was the destiny of woman, and the celebrations that attended the rites were the crowning days of her early life.

The Education of Boys

Boys were destined for another way of life: a career in business or banking, or a profession as notary or judge. In his infancy, as was the custom, a boy would be provided with a wet nurse. Morelli's father, in the fourteenth century, remembered his wet nurse with passionate hatred as a woman who often beat him. Past infancy, it was not unusual for a son to serve an apprenticeship with some merchant while learning his reading, his writing, and his arithmetic. Mazzei was especially concerned about the education of his boys, anxious that Piero should have his abacus, that he should have the opportunity to work off his animal spirits among his own age group at school. His anguish over the death of his oldest son, who had begun to make great strides in his career by being employed in the Ardingo Bank, does much to rectify the impression of family relationships always severe and lacking in affection: "God knows how much hope this oldest boy was to me . . . ."

Those of the merchant class were anxious for their sons to acquire some knowledge of trade, but Paolo da Certaldo advises parents to guide their children into an art or skill which is in keeping with their endowments. "Boys," he writes, "cannot all be of the same mind . . . ask each what trade or calling he wishes to pursue. . . . In this he will attain some mastery; more than if you had forced him into something you preferred." And like Cecco Angiolieri (*ca.* 1260–1312) he warns against inadvertently alienating a child from his homeland by sending him abroad to learn his trade: "Say not, I will send my boy as a child to France to grow up and learn a trade there . . . because when he . . . returns to Florence, he will never be a good Guild member . . . and his heart will always be in France."

Villani, among the great amount of detail which he has bequeathed to us, relates that in 1338 there were in Florence's lower schools, out of a population of about 90,000 souls, between 8,000 and 10,000 children of both sexes learning to read. Boys put to learning arithmetic and "algorism" numbered between 1,000 and 1,200. From 550 to 600 were studying grammar, logic—that is, Latin—and the basic elements of philosophy, in five or six different schools. The elementary instruction was in the hands of private teachers who, after the opening years of the fourteenth century, were exempted from taxes, an indication of the small returns they earned from their students. A better opportunity for the individual teacher was to become a part of a rich household and there become the tutor of the children. Most of the early instruction was, at least through the thirteenth century, given by the clergy; after this time there are references to lay teachers, among them women, taking the children at the age of six and keeping them under their tutelage for five years.

From age eleven to age thirteen or fourteen, boys might

103

receive special training in business arithmetic before going on as apprentices in the world of industry and business, learning the new system of Arabic numbers which was then competing with the older Roman system, and gradually learning to equate Florentine prices with those of distant cities with which the merchants dealt.

Florence may boast of its Latin instruction, using Donatus as a basis; its teachers of Latin show up in Bologna and Venice. Boccaccio, Filippo Villani tells us, learned his Latin from Giovanni da Strada, father of Zanobi, poet laureate who in his turn also taught Latin. By 1339 four schools teaching Latin—that is, basic Virgil, Seneca, and Boethius —were in existence. More practically, the student's knowledge of Latin had to be sufficiently sound to enable him to read legal documents and contracts, as well as to write a letter in that language. Petrarch himself was taught by the ancient Ser Convenevole da Prato, a former judge and notary, who at the age of seventy-six (1336) was still teaching Cicero and the intricacies of rhetoric.

Rhetoric also served a more immediate function: the preparation of men in public life for political occasions demanding persuasive speech in the vernacular tongue. This included embassies, as well as the more ordinary but more important influencing of legislation in the councils of the commune, and the addresses to the people from the platforms outside the Palazzo della Signoria.

Morelli, in his *Chronicle* written at the end of the fourteenth century, speaking for an upper class, mentions schools of music, of dancing, and of fencing. These, he advises, should be enjoyed in times not given to more serious scholarly pursuits. Morelli seriously defends learning past the school level. He suggests a reading of "Virgil, Boethius,

Seneca and others." The result will be great exercise of the mind and presence of mind in the affairs of life. The difficulties of early training in the classics, though troublesome at first, he writes, give way to the pleasures of knowledge, sufficient to inculcate an indifference to riches, family, and station. Virgil, Boethius, Dante, Cicero, and Aristotle (in Latin translation) will teach one how to live above the affairs of life. And in the reading of the Bible, with its story of the great plan of God and in the account of Jesus, "you will have great consolation of the spirit, great joy, a great sweetness, contempt for the world, and trust of the future."

That Latin was difficult Dante himself tells us in a rare passage of the *Convivio* (ii, 13), where he says he learned to read Boethius and Cicero "with the aid of his *spirito divinatore.*" When he was already twenty-six, he frequented the schools of the religious to listen to the discussions of philosophical problems, studying with them for two and a half years. Whether this was at the *studium* of the Dominican Santa Maria Novella or that of the Franciscan Santa Croce, or even at the Augustinian Santo Spirito he does not say. And whether his remark, *"cominciai ad andare . . . ne le scuole deli religiosi e a le disputazioni deli filosofanti,"* refers to two distinct disciplines is not entirely clear. In any case he would have been exposed to the intellectual system of St. Thomas at Santa Maria Novella under such a teacher as Remigio Girolami, a graduate of Paris, and to the *Sententiae* of Peter Lombard. The Dominicans there, in spite of strictures against reading the works of Dante, nonetheless applied themselves to his works, and within a few brief decades we find the Orcagna brothers depicting both the Paradise and the Inferno, in Dante's scheme, upon the walls of the Strozzi Chapel.

The disputations to which Dante refers would have been an exciting debate or discussion over philosophical matters, sometimes restricted in audience to students, but other times open to the public. Here Dante himself could have participated in the discussions, raising questions and objections, and meeting at such convocations the intellectuals of his time. In this sense, the disputations would be distinguished from his more basic studies in the religious schools which included Donatus and Priscian in Latin, logic, and the works of Aristotle, from which Dante was subsequently to draw so much of his learning.

Dante's traditional associations with the Franciscans cannot be shrugged off as a mere possibility. Of a mystical bent, with almost a Platonic insistence upon the apperception of the Eternal through an ecstatic union, their influence may account for much in the spiritual sweetness that overrides the moral schematism of the *Divine Comedy* and blends love with knowledge in it. It was at Santa Croce that Pietro Olivi (*ca.* 1248–98) and Ubertino da Casale (1259–*ca.* 1338), two well-known Franciscans, were in all likelihood heard by Dante.

From this point on in the education of the humanist or professional of Dante's century and beyond, higher studies, when they were not available in Florence itself, could be pursued in the famous universities of Bologna and Paris, or even Oxford; we note, however, good schools strewn throughout Italy, like Pistoia, Siena, Padua, and Arezzo (until 1373). Young men away from home constitute a mixed blessing for parents of the time, and we hear much of student vices, both from the Goliardic songs and from historical records. Tales of debauchery, thievery, wild parties, and even murder plagued the hearts of parents who must have earlier consoled themselves with the thought of great teachers of theology, law, or medicine, under whom their offspring would increase in wisdom.

The Vanities

The picture of women in the home, under the strict guard of their husbands, confined to the narrow existence of rearing their children, is not entirely true. A different story is told in the Sumptuary laws and in the tirades of the preachers against the folly of women. But life was short, and women maintained their reputation for making Florence renowned for its lovely ladies by all sorts of tricks and dodges.

The ideal of beauty being the French Gothic, particular attention was paid to coiffure, to eyebrows, to complexion, and to color of hair. Those who were not blonde by nature bleached their hair, using various corrosive substances, or stood in the sun wearing special crownless hats to protect their complexions while exposing their locks. Although this was thought to be damaging to the brain and a peril to the soul, women passed "the whole day upon the housetops, some curling their hair, some smoothing it, some bleaching it, until they died of pneumonia." And if dyes and sun could not make one over into a modish blonde, there were other remedies: the moonlight was thought to help, or special large-toothed ivory combs. Then as now, hairdressers and beauticians offered their assistance for removing superfluous hair and for hair-styling, as Boccaccio tells us in the *Corbaccio*. Even San Bernardino complained later that women had become self-flayers, plucking their eyebrows and their hairline as well.

The complexion was a matter of special interest, and pale skin the rage. Various washes were employed, the water drawn from propitious wells and boiled; into these were mixed dilutions made from roses or lilies. The skin could be kept soft by means of unguents made of chemicals or animal blood. Over the ladies' tender skins went various powders and ointments, so that Boccaccio could complain that they smeared the lips of their lovers with salves when they kissed.

Taddeo Gaddi and Albert Arnoldi, in a story of Sacchetti's, agreed that Florentine women were the best artists in the world, both in painting and in sculpture: "Was there ever a painter who put white upon black, or turned white into black, except these? There is born many a maiden, perhaps most of them, who looks like a beetle. They rub them here, they chalk them there, they put them in the sun and make them grow whiter than a bean. And what artist is there, what painter, what dyer, who can turn black into white? Certainly not one, for it is against nature. Yet should there be a pale and yellow face, by using artificial colors, the women make it into the likeness of a rose. She who through defects of age appears withered is made blooming and plump. I do not except Giotto or any other painter when I say that none applies color as well as these women."

So much for the painter's art. As for sculpture: "Even more important, a badly proportioned face with protruding eyes is straightway as well groomed as a falcon. If the nose is crooked, they straighten it; if the jaws are like those of a mule, they adjust them. If the shoulders are too high, they flatten them, and if one is higher than the other they level them with padding so that they are proportioned and adjusted. And so with the breast, achieving without a chisel what Polycletus himself could not have achieved with one."

It is a favorite refrain among preachers and moralists,

too, well on into the fifteenth century, and Alberti's dialogue relates how the father of the family gently reduced his wife to tears as he persuaded her not to paint and rouge her face: "I am sorry to see that you've got your face plastered; have you stuck it against some pan in the kitchen? . . . a woman who is the mistress of a family should always be clean. I left her," he says, "to wash away her paint and tears, and never needed to speak to her again on the matter." It is a return to that persistent strain of complaint which makes the cosmetic arts a sign of a degenerate age. Cacciaguida's golden age, we recall, was one in which men saw their ladies "turn away from the mirror" with face unpainted.

Dante and Villani both assert that Florence used to be sober and modest and that its women were not, like the women of their day, bedecked with jewelry, ornate headdresses, and waistbands which attracted more attention than the person wearing them. In their day, fashions had become so immodest that the Church would soon censure the daring styles from the pulpit. Women of Florence, Dante has Forese Donati say, are so brazen that they wear dresses exposing their breasts.

The extravagances in dress were but a symptom of the changing economy of the time and the widening of the social horizons made possible by the world of trade. How seriously shall we take the charges of a progressive degeneration in taste and morals? In the very period which writers exalt for its sobriety and rude simplicity the Sumptuary laws of Cardinal Latino for the year 1240 prohibit trains on the female dress. These trains, says Salimbene, were dearer to women than all the rest of the garment. The alternative offered them by the preachers, if they chose to persist in folly, was to go unshriven. The choice that women made individually we can see from the persistence of the train. Even the veils that women were enjoined to wear for modesty soon became a moral peril rather than a moral safeguard. Made of linen and silk with gold threads woven through them, they increased the allure of women tenfold and *"magis ad lasciviam videntium oculos attrahebant."*

The enactment of Sumptuary laws in the fourteenth and fifteenth centuries makes it perfectly clear that women and their fashions were really a great trial to lawmakers. Villani tells us that Florentine women were actually setting the styles for other cities of Tuscany. To be sure, these laws were aimed at restricting excessive spending on other matters: dowry, trousseau, marriage feasts, funeral celebrations, and the like. But their principal target was female dress: ornaments of all sorts, headdresses, garlands, and nets and wreaths of gold, silver, and pearl. Women were particularly daring in headpieces and in the styling of the dress itself, progressively lowering necklines, widening sleeves, and lengthening the train. Their hair, when not covered by pearl-and-ribbon nets, was sprinkled with gold dust to make it glisten. Where their own hair was insufficient, they adopted curls and braids taken from the dead.

The battle between the law and women has amusing vicissitudes. In 1326 when Charles, duke of Calabria, was *signore* of Florence, he was prevailed upon by his wife, Marie de Valois, to restore to the women of Florence an ornament dear to their hearts, a yellow and white silk braid. It was, to Villani, an immodest and unnatural thing. "Thus does the disordinate appetite of women overcome the reason and the judgment of men," he writes, and takes considerable care in describing minutely the restrictions imposed

110

upon women in 1330, after the death of Charles and the war of Castruccio.

In 1342, when the nefarious Duke of Athens came to Florence, he followed the example of Charles of Calabria. Among the indignities visited upon the city, he restored all their ornaments to the women. And in 1348, the terrible year that the Plague devastated Florence, contemporary writers are agreed that the terror of the time produced a general deterioration of moral fiber. Matteo Villani describes the time as one when men gave themselves up to a shameful life, to gluttony, to the lusts of the flesh, and to new and strange fashions.

Sacchetti himself can assume the tone of complaint: "Young women who used to dress modestly . . . go dressed like common women. . . . And what more wretched, dangerous, and useless style ever existed than that of wearing such sleeves, or rather sacks, as they do? They cannot raise a glass or take a mouthful without soiling both their sleeves and the table cloth by upsetting the glasses on the table . . . truly there would be no end of describing the garb of these women, and the extravagance of their dress from head to toe. . . . Oh vanity!"

It must be admitted that men also offended, and liked fancy display as well as women. They wore fine brocades, velvets, and silks. Their stockings were parti-colored. They wore hoods and ruffs and wristbands so ridiculous that they looked as if they had on "water pipes around their necks and tiles on their arms." Young men did away with mantles and wore their hair long. They further simplified their garb by wearing pants and hose so tight that they could hardly sit down. Their shoes were long and pointed, says Sacchetti, and their legs wrapped with laces. Sometimes they wore tight-fitting jackets with wristbands lined with ermine, and tunics belted with fancy leather and buckle. Many of these details of both male and female dress may be seen in the frescoes of the time, particularly in those of the Spanish Chapel at Santa Maria Novella.

All of these garments were subject to an infinite variety of change according to the dictates of successive styles brought in from France, Germany, or Hungary. They were a far cry from that simplicity which Dante praises in Bellincion Berti. But it must be remembered that the complaints against luxury in men are less frequent than those against women. Their gowns with trains, their detachable sleeves, their great variety of headdresses caused San Bernardino to devote the better part of six long sermons against the folly of women and the "disgraceful and disgusting" fashions "so spread abroad in Italy in my time." One can only admire the instinct for the beautiful in the lesser arts, even when it manifests itself in extravagances that trouble the moralist. It was in all likelihood a rebellion against much that is grim in the life of the century.

The truth of human experience, that generalizations about women are perilous, should make us wary of the old proverb cited by Francesco da Barberino that a good as well as a bad woman needs a beating. That money and sensuality are woman's driving motives Chaucer in England and Boccaccio in Italy both assert. But we must remember that patient Griselda is the crowning feminine portrait of both writers. It is unfortunate that we do not have from the period the written views of women answering the charges so often lodged against them. Their opinions about what was in many ways a thankless and difficult life, the burdensome and endless succession of children, the casually accepted adultery

112

by men, the bastard children sired on slave girls who were part of the household, would give us pause. And anyone who has read the charges and harangues of the preachers, for whom they formed the principal audience, must admire their patience and their ability to withstand a tremendous amount of mental cruelty. That time worked its ravages on the most beautiful of them we can be sure. Sacchetti, at the close of one of the tales, says sadly that within a short time they "drooped, declined and withered into old age."

6. *Up at a Villa*—*Down in the City*

ONE OF THE HAPPIER ASPECTS of Florentine life in the thirteenth and fourteenth centuries may be seen in the passion for the land indulged by the wealthy and near-wealthy, with their beloved *case di campagna*. As we have seen earlier, in the gradual widening of the city, the walls pressed close upon the surrounding countryside. Indeed, at every stage of the city's development we read of farms, of orchards, of gardens. Even today, a ride of but a few minutes brings one into the beautiful hills and valleys of the Tuscan countryside, with its neat rows of trees and vines and its carefully cultivated plots of ground.

Just as noble and peasant alike had come to the city over the course of the eleventh and twelfth centuries, so in the subsequent century we find the rich as well as the commoner moving back to the cherished land, if only a few acres of stony ground on the side of a hill. The houses of the *petite bourgeoisie* and the newly rich surrounded Florence with the beauty that comes not only from love but from the competitive spirit with which the newly wealthy built their houses to vaunt their riches. Beyond the beauties of the city itself, writes Villani, "there wasn't a citizen, common or rich, who had not built or was in the process of building in the country a large, rich estate and grounds, with buildings on it more beautiful than these in town. Everyone was guilty, and on account of the great expenditures was thought insane."

114

Boccaccio, in the *Decameron,* describes one such beautiful house and grounds (Introduction to Day I and III), with courtyard and flower-bedecked upper loggia, with gardens artfully planted in roses and other flowers, with blooming orange and lemon trees perfuming the air, and with a fountain and sculptures adorning the park. We cannot deny that Boccaccio's description is based upon fact, however transformed by poetic imagination.

In the summer such a dwelling must have provided a welcome change for the fortunate "mad" ones who had escaped from the evil odors of the city. It was an age, we must remember, when slops were cast out into the lanes or alleys between houses. And plumbing—if we may call it such—although common in the houses of the rich under a variety of names, was of course lacking in those of the lower classes. In town a statute of 1325 forbade the debouching of wastes upon streets or public piazzas, and it was advised that all owners of *stanzette* build covered canals by which wastes could reach the river—an ideal situation, however impractical. But residents of medieval Florence continued to empty their wastes in the alleys, taking their permitted week to clean them up when annoyed neighbors complained.

The escape to the country is a favorite subject in the memoranda and letters of the fourteenth century. Even the wealthy Giotto rode out weekly to his farm to oversee its affairs, willing to put up with inconvenience and bad weather, typically Tuscan in his attachment to the land. Practically speaking, it is clear that many of the farms were poor, and that the city-dweller's interest in his farm was a realistic one, representing an investment of money on which he wished a return. Many landowners, not able to run their

115

farms themselves, being weekend visitors so to speak, resorted in the fourteenth century to the *mèzzadría,* or profit-sharing system. In it the owner guaranteed to his farmworkers a house and tools, seed, and cattle, in return for —he hoped—honest labor and half the profits. This arrangement, although it has persisted in many parts of the world, raised many problems. Paolo da Certaldo, not very happy with the workers, and clearly distrustful of them, could cite an old proverb, "The country produces good animals and bad men," and advise against consorting with the shrewd peasants until they have expended their energies by hard work at plow and shovel. On their home ground, he complains, they band together against the landowner, who better settles accounts with them one by one in the city.

For Lapo Mazzei, however, satisfied with a few fields and a small orchard, the country was a source of that serenity which colors so many of his letters. In them we begin to see something of the idyllic and the purely literary blurring of the harsher realities. But Mazzei's sincerity is unquestionable. He watched his friend Datini acquire lands and properties in Prato, Florence, Pistoia, and Pisa, and work at them with frenzy, eliciting from Lapo the warning that concern for property had become a peril to his soul. "I call my place a garden, because a place so small cannot be called a farm. But for my modest tastes it is big enough. This faculty of not desiring overmuch seems to me the height of riches." And again, "Hold me excused for not coming to stay with you. Friday, like a man angry at nothing, I staked and tied up the vines." Mazzei could not wait to escape from the burdens of his job in town, going by horse to his plot of ground where in blessed solitude he would loaf and invite his soul. With fourteen children over the course of the years, the farm must have seemed a haven of peace. Here, and at the villa of his friend Guido del Palagio, he read his beloved Boethius, St. Jerome, the Gospels, the *Laudi* of Jacopone da Todi, the *Fioretti* of St. Francis, and other books of devotion.

The most glowing paean in honor of the pastoral life we owe to Alberti. A summary of many views current in the fourteenth century, it is more purely a literary tradition going back to classical antiquity. It is a long recitation of the virtues of country living, season after season, month after month. To it are contrasted the evils of city life, with its dissensions and cheating injustice.

And as we read in it of the open skies, verdant plains, those fountains, and the streams leaping down the hills, the beauty of the description blinds us momentarily to the sweat and labor of the poor peasant for whom San Bernardino pleaded, by whose efforts the gracious life was made possible. Still it is a welcome change from much that is grim in the life of the Florentine, a reminder that the good life was attained by some, in that age-old debate between the city and the country. It is a side of life that Chaucer managed to suggest in his white-bearded Franklin, a character not vastly different from the old patriarch Agnolo Pandolfini (b.1360), described by his biographer Vespasian da Bisticci as "another Lucullus." Like Chaucer's Franklin, his house near Florence was provided with every sort of fine food for his guests. And if after a hawking he had no guests, his servants brought wayfarers off the roads into the house where "water was given them to wash their hands" before dinner. It was a gentleman's world of dogs, hawks, fishing, and horses, more suggestive of a romantic ideal than of the less colorful reality. But as we know, the age was one of contrasts, of happiness and misery, of wealth and poverty, of villainy and sanctity, and the historical records are too full of both for us to deny the one or the other.

† † †

Yet in Florence life was not always grim. Her citizens always managed to find time for play, in a more natural use of the energies which they poured into their factional struggles. Some of their activities were purely social, like endless conversation and the simpler games of ball played by women and men alike, and the not-so-simple game of tennis. Other games, innocent in intention, became violent and quarrelsome, like the various types of dice and cards.

Chess has an ancient history in Florentine annals, going back to the eleventh century. Even Villani records an incident in which in 1266 the Saracen Buzzecca, the great chess master, played in the presence of Guido Novello, in the newly completed Palazzo del Podesta, three games of chess simultaneously with the finest players of the city. Two of the games he played "blind," the other with the board in sight, winning two of the games and drawing the other. And in the fourteenth century there appeared in Florence a collection of chess problems, based on an earlier Spanish "Good Companion"; and other collections were well known. As a gambling game, frequently accompanied by extensive drinking, it drew various censures. Dante forecasts the death of one Riccardo da Camino, killed by his enemies as he sat concentrating upon his game (*Par.* ix 47ff.), and there are other such instances recorded in the fourteenth century. Sacchetti relates a happier tale in which Guido Cavalcanti, playing a losing game, is teased by an obstreperous child. The boy nails Guido's cloak to the bench and makes his escape while Guido waits to get loose.

Games of dice were common and enticing. Boccaccio, Dante, and Sacchetti all attest, with the preachers, to the great temptation to the spirit that dice and tables afforded. Treated principally as a vice because it wasted the substance of life and went hand in hand with various forms of extravagance, gambling was sometimes a source of income to the commune. Some cities provided houses of play called *baratterie,* with *barattieri* in the employ of the city. Florence did not have such official houses, as did Siena, Lucca, Bologna, and Faenza, among others, using the gambler-proprietors for various other tasks, like scourging prisoners and collecting taxes. Florence made its money from taxing or fining those who violated the laws against gambling, employing spies to ferret out gamesters. These could not have been difficult to find, for they played their games around the Baptistry, various other churches, and in the safer wilds of the Mercato Vecchio.

The games were not restricted to the commoners. On the contrary, the religious and professionals, the common soldiers, the knights, the merchants all were smitten from time to time with the passion for play. The *barattieri* were apparently considered part of the armed forces, and Villani describes them as having an ensign of their own: a group of *barattieri* playing, on a white background.

In a memorable metaphor in the *Divine Comedy,* Dante describes the close of a game in which the winner of a game of Zara goes off surrounded by hindering admirers, while the loser goes off sadder and wiser, replaying plays. The game of Zara, played with three dice, consisted of call-

119

ing a number at the moment of throw, with the hope of matching the call with the total appearing on the dice, and of avoiding the lowest and highest combinations, which were called *zare*.

Popular among the more vigorous males of Florentine —as well as Milanese, Perugian, Sienese—society were various jousts, like running at targets; a form of the ancient *hastiludium,* these consisted of displays of skillful horsemanship, usually presented in the Piazza dei Priori on festive occasions before delighted spectators. More brutal were the various games of Pugna and Ponte, given many names indicating equipment necessary for play: bats, helmets, shields, clubs, and the like. The teams were drawn up on the basis of parish, or guild, or locale, and pitted against each other "for fun." The teams could run to great numbers, and in the melee, violence often produced smashed heads, damaged noses, split lips, and broken teeth. The games of Ponte were specifically those in which a mock battle was held between squadrons or companies defending a bridge site, and as in the more splendid games of Pugna, the squads —at least those of Pisa—were equipped with colors and banners. There were attempts to eradicate the more brutal aspects of the games, but the fourteenth century retained them nonetheless as a means of working off some of their violent energies.

On these games, as well as on tourneys and jousts, Dante is silent. His silence is a sign of an aloofness from all that is extravagant and unbridled. More to his taste, apparently, at least as a sort of simile, is hunting, a sport of the wealthy. We remember the gruesome details of the boar hunt in the forest of suicides and spendthrifts, and those of the wolf hunt in the dream of Ugolino. A great many images he draws from bird life; in one of them he speaks impatiently of those who waste their lives peering into green foliage. Falconry was, of course, a noble sport and art, and some of Dante's more powerful images are drawn from this subject. In Dante's time, when the environs of Florence and the slopes of the hills had not been entirely denuded of tree cover and brush, wild life abounded, and hunting was not only a sport but a self-protective measure. Villani tells of a wolf which entered the city (in 1345) on the south side of the river, through the Porta San Giorgio, and was not killed until it reached the other end of town, the Porta San Frediano. Later in the century both Boccaccio and Sacchetti base stories upon encounters with wolves.

Within the city social life, both among the upper classes and among the people, was organized into "brigades," their aim being the pursuit of pleasure. Their immediate purpose was feasting, music, and dancing. One such company was made up of one thousand or more men who wore white garments, and had as their leader one whom they called the "Lord of Love." His tour of duty or "court" lasted two months. It was a powerful attraction for the jesters, who were richly received. To these we must add other grades of entertainment, like the buffoons, the mimics, the jugglers, and the tumblers who congregated to the companies of fun lovers. From Lombardy and all of Italy they came, says Villani, to help in whatever celebration was afoot, usually for some visiting person of note who was provided with escort by the brigade.

The particular company of the Lord of Love described by Villani came into existence in the district of Santa Felicita, south of the Arno, on the occasion of the Feast of St. John in 1283, and it was followed by a number of others.

121

Dante mentions a Sienese group known as the Spendthrift Club in disparaging terms. But Boccaccio in his time laments that the brigades have disappeared. These, he recalls, met at least once a year in their uniforms, and on special days rode in processions through town, holding jousts, and entertaining lavishly. The club that operated under the leadership of Betto Brunelleschi (killed in 1311 as he sat at chess) sought to enlist Guido Cavalcanti as a member not so much for his intellectual abilities but for his courtesy and—an essential—his money.

Of the groups made up of commoner folk, the dependable Villani records that in the year 1304 the companies were revived. One from the Borgo San Frediano which had the reputation for doing novel things announced for Calendimaggio a specialty: whoever wished to have news of the other world must be at or on the Carraia bridge. In spirit of fun crowds thronged the bridge to see the various scenes from hell which were presented on floats: demons torturing poor souls amidst "fires and other pains and punishments." Under the crushing weight of the populace the bridge collapsed and many persons drowned. In much of his reporting Villani sees the excesses of the companies as invitations to the wrath of God. But the brigades continued throughout the century, both among the commoners and the wealthy, under the auspices of a succession of rulers of Florence.

May Day, with its processions of pretty girls, its songs and dances, and its queen-for-a-day in her chariot, was a favorite holiday in Florence. Brigades of young men and women ushered in the season with decorated booths, and dancing and dining. The festivities from time to time ended with fisticuffs and, by nightfall, with factions of the city in arms. At one neighborhood banquet of this festive season,

Dante, then nine, first set eyes upon the daughter of Folco Portinari, the beloved Beatrice.

Even more exciting to the Florentine taste was the Feast of St. John, on June 24. Primarily a religious holiday honoring the patron of the city, it was also a social occasion with street dances and the exciting race called the Pálio. The piazza between the Baptistry and the cathedral was sheltered from the sun by a canopy of blue cloth on which were sewn great yellow lilies and great circles bearing the various insignia of the commune. From the edges hung banners bearing the ensigns of the various guilds. The whole canopy was suspended about forty feet from the ground by ropes tied to irons in the walls of the two churches.

The two-day religious holiday featured a clerical procession, with exposition of the relics of the church, and the offering of candles or a length of rich cloth by the various guilds and important citizens. The wax and cloth not used by the church were sold, the proceeds to be used for the various art works of the Baptistry; over the course of the century the gifts of cloth became more and more splendid, and the profit was considerable. On the feast day, mass was celebrated with music. In the afternoon, the great race was held for the prize of a strip of cloth called the *palio*.

The race itself, referred to by Dante's ancestor as "your annual game," was not of ancient lineage, although it was well established by Dante's lifetime. Before the race started, the prize, usually of a rich red stuff, was carried upon a triumphal car drawn by two horses. The prize, worth up to 300 or more florins, merited such treatment, and the trappings on horse and riders leading the chariot were extravagant and gay.

When the bell in the tower of the Palazzo della Signoria

had rung three times, the race was on; the race horses and riders started from the western edge of the city, passed through the Borgo Ognissanti, crossed the center of town through the Mercato Vecchio, then went by way of the Corso to the eastern part of the city. There the first arrival received his prize from the hands of a lovely lady, while trumpeters hailed his victory. As the climax to the festival of St. John, the race naturally merited great attention. Flowers banked the streets on which it took place, the houses along the way displaying their finest tapestries, and women in finery thronged the thoroughfare.

When Florence was at war, the horse races were run in the fields. The *patio*, instead of being displayed on a chariot, was suspended from a pole carried by a horseman. Such games seem to have served as a gesture of contempt in the face of a defeated or beleagured enemy. The Pisans ran such a race in 1264 outside the walls of Lucca, and the Florentines, during the siege of Arezzo in 1289, carrying on their celebration of St. John's day, not only ran a Palio but threw slaughtered asses with miters on their heads "in scorn of the Bishops there" into the city. And in 1325, Castruccio, then ruler of Lucca, after routing the Florentines, not only devastated the countryside, but had three races run: one on horseback, one on foot, and a third by the prostitutes drawn from his camp followers. Five years later the Florentines returned the compliment to the Lucchese. Still later, in 1363, the Pisans repeated the indignities against the Florentines in exactly the same way, adding further refinements: they suspended three dead asses bearing the names of prominent Florentines on the gallows near the walls of the city.

7. The Three Crowns of Tuscany

DANTE HIMSELF COINED THE TERM "the sweet new style," to describe the subject and expression of poems of which he and Guido Cavalcanti were the most efficient practitioners. Their "father" in this literary movement had been the Bolognese Guido Guinicelli (1230?–75?), a poet who had managed in Dante's view to refine the language of their region and to elevate it until it became adequate for their special subject matter, the psychology of love.

This topic of discussion, stemming originally from the poets of Provence who had disseminated their influence over Italy and principally in Sicily, had found a spokesman in Guittone d' Arezzo (1225?–93), a poet whom Dante later condemned as falling short of the demands of an appropriate diction and form. The subject of the Provençal poets and then of those whom they influenced had been the exaltation of a beloved woman, the sorrows of unfulfilled aspiration, the failure of human reason. Now, in the Tuscan poets and principally in Dante and his "first friend" Guido Cavalcanti, love becomes more than a debilitating passion: it is the source of nobility, the purifier of base emotions, a manifestation of the divine in human affairs. "When Love speaks, I listen, and what he awakens in my heart I utter to men." So writes Dante of his inspiration, calling attention to an incorruptible sincerity of expression which he felt essential to the subject of his poems.

Not all of the poetry of the age was of this rarefied sort. Some of it was railing, bitter, realistic. Cecco Angiolieri in Siena, with whom Dante exchanged some sonnets, was writing rancorous poems about his father, or about the delights of gambling and tavern life. But Dante was, as a young writer, mining his new-found subject, the love song, and making it the record of his spiritual development. Love was for him a center holding all around it in precise relationships. The beloved was a type of supreme beatitude, and as such the goal of man's inner life. So noble a subject naturally demanded a style adequate to its elevated meaning.

The work into which the youthful Dante collected his poems, giving them a new significance by setting them into a prose frame, is the *Vita Nuova*. In its underlying metaphor, what is "new" is the illumination of a hitherto undiscovered life to which love, by purifying him, has allowed him to progress. It is, in the last analysis, a religious experience, in which Beatrice is an angel and an instrument in Dante's salvation, and hence a form of grace. All of Dante's youthful poems are not here, inasmuch as some of them were for reasons of artistry rigorously excluded from the collection. In the self-conscious act of bringing the suitable ones together Dante was, with the independence of a rapidly developing genius, purging the sweet new style of much that was merely conventional, ridding a pagan Amor of its entirely sensual elements, and moving toward the philosophy of love which would find its mature expression in the great poem by which posterity chiefly remembers him.

Dante's love for Beatrice had a historical basis. But her human existence and her higher reality in Paradise soon take on an allegorical cast. The work is best approached as a sublime fiction in which the simple events become the

126

vehicle by which the lovers' spiritual progress is charted. Thus the conventions of a courtly love, the bedazzlement of his senses in her presence, Beatrice's misunderstanding of his attentions to other women, all serve some other purpose. This purpose is implicated with a Biblical tone, a suggestive number symbolism, and the gradual amalgamation of Beatrice into a heavenly being, all crystallizing into the theme of love and its educative force in man's religious experience.

With the death of Beatrice, Dante turned to studies, in particular to Cicero and Boethius. Florence was at this time burgeoning with schools for both clerics and laity, principally at Santa Maria Novella, Santa Croce, and Santo Spirito, and Dante frequented their discussions. The fruit of his reading and his study was to be seen throughout his intellectual life in the frequent references not merely to philosophers but to the poets of antiquity. He was in the process of casting off the limitations of love-service under the profounder influences of the great writers. At the same time he was in the process of entering into the political life of his times.

The events underway after 1290 gradually absorbed him into the turbulent political career of the city. He had already, according to Bruni, fought as a cavalryman in the battle of Campaldino (1289). When democratic reform finally allowed the aristocracy to participate in local government, Dante fulfilled the requirement by enrolling himself in a guild which attracted intellectuals, that of physicians and apothecaries. For the remaining years of his life in Florence he actively engaged himself in a variety of councils, acting on matters of importance to the Guelf league in Tuscany, and in 1300, served the two-month term of duty as prior.

It was a time of great civic strife, a time when it was necessary for Florence to keep strong ties with its neighbors against the ambitious claims of Boniface Viii, anxious to bring the wealthy commune and all of Tuscany under his control. Dino Compagni has described on almost a day-to-day basis the catastrophe brewing in the two factions of the Guelf party, the aristocratic Blacks led by the powerful baron Corso Donati, who hoped by allegiance to the Pope to restore the influence of his family in the commune; and the rich merchant Whites under the vacillating banker Vieri de' Cerchi, who hoped to maintain the independence of the city. Dante was aristocratic by birth, but his passionate regard for Florentine independence drew him to the White faction.

Florence was caught between the pressures of the Donati and the papal see. The Pope himself, after overtures to the Whites, found an ideal co-operator in Corso and in the French prince, Charles of Valois, whom he had instructed to subdue first Sicily and then Tuscany. One negative vote by Dante in council against continuing the practice of sending an auxiliary force of one hundred soldiers to the Pope enables us to estimate the degree to which he was now confirmed in his attitudes toward the Pontiff.

As Charles drew near the city, promising to be a peace-maker, Dante was, according to Dino, chosen to be one of three to go to the court of Boniface to arbitrate. He was not, apparently, in Florence when on November 1, Charles entered the city, and in almost open co-operation with the Blacks under Corso, allowed the wholesale plunder and burning of the city and the suppression of White leadership. According to Dino, Dante was retained at the court of Boniface so he was absent when the first sentence was lodged against him on January 27, 1302: a fine of 5,000 small florins, payable in three days, or confiscation of all properties, banishment for two years under the general charge of malfeasance in office, extortion, and opposition to the cause of the Pope in Florence and Pistoia. On March 10 another decree appeared, assuming Dante's guilt and condemning him to death by burning if he should fall into the control of the city.

From that time on, Dante remained in exile lamenting his inability to return to the city—not the people—he loved. Love of one's own city-state, we recall, had a more pressing reality than it does for other times and places owing to a variety of political, social, and cultural reasons. But from the suffering, the disillusionment with factional politics, and his travels through northern Italy virtually as a beggar dependent upon the patronage of various great families in Verona, in Lunigiana, and in Ravenna, come the refinement of his political ideas and the gradual formulation of a political philosophy which is to coalesce in the great poem with his religious views.

The first of the works in exile, the *Convivio,* is a fragment of an encyclopedia which was intended to cover fifteen books, fourteen of which were to be commentaries on a long poem. It was to make available a great range of information for those men and women caught up in the affairs of life who could here learn better how to adapt themselves to the daily challenge. Keeping in mind those who must perform important functions, he pointedly excludes the learned who have, in his view, debased their calling, and writes in the vernacular for those on whom social well-being depends. He includes women as necessary to a stable social system, and as the preservers of custom and the sources of virtue.

129

The philosophy to which he leads his readers is that of Aristotle, filtered through St. Thomas. To him the Greek was the "glorious philosopher to whom nature revealed her secrets more than to any other." From him, and from a host of others, he emphasizes over and over again the function of philosophy to give, beyond wisdom, a rule of life, an improvement of the emotions, a correction of the disordered soul and mind of man. Philosophy, it becomes clear, has taken the place of love, and the meaning has slightly changed, but in motivation and directive power they are essentially the same.

Especially interesting to students of literature, too, is the discussion of the allegorical or fourfold interpretation of poetry. In Dante's summation of the tradition he offers four senses of interpretation: a literal or narrative level which is fundamental to the others; then the first of the "hidden" levels, called "allegory," in which we discern the truth built upon belief or religious conviction; then a moral level, which has to do with the conduct of life; and finally a level called "anagogy" which has to do with the progress or destiny of the soul. Such was the method used to interpret Scripture, and with discretion it may be applied to poetry. Far from new with Dante, the method had been in use from most ancient times, and in the very early Middle Ages had been employed to interpret the *Aeneid*. Dante takes the system of Scripture, and while recognizing difficulties in the gradations of thought represented by the various levels, applies it to his own *Canzoni* in the *Convivio*.

In order to reach the opponents of the vernacular Dante wrote, sometime around 1305, a treatise in Latin, on the Italian language. Like the *Convivio,* it is unfinished. Dante failed to get beyond the fourteenth chapter of the second book. He had intended at least four books. He had in mind a full discussion of language, but after a rapid classification of the various dialects—a valuable contribution to philology —he moves into the subject of an ideal tongue for Italy, a language stripped of defects and dialectal differences, and finally into a discussion of the language and subjects of poetry.

The dialects are in his view all defective, even Tuscan and Florentine. By the process of elimination and comparison, he finds traces of the best vernacular throughout the regions of Italy, mainly in the poets, until he attains by such process the ideal national language. He works constantly from the literary to the common language rather than from the common language to the literary, being convinced that the dialects are corruptions of the pre-existing more ideal forms. It is a scholastic and perhaps ultimately Neo-Platonic process through which he passes, but it serves to point up a sense of race which Dante felt poignantly, the conviction that there was a basic language for Italy. This nationalism is manifested in other ways, too—in the insistence that Italy should be united under one ruler, as in fact, according to his view, it was already one in language and social custom.

The second book, a kind of *Poetics,* attributes the ideal language only to the best writers. He then proceeds to the discussion of the subjects best suited to this language, namely love, war, and virtue. These require the high or tragic style as distinguished from the comic and elegiac styles, and the literary form best suited to them, in this case the *canzone* rather than the ballad or sonnet.

The *Convivio* and the *De Vulgari Eloquentia* were works begun in the early painful period of wandering; both of them refer to the anguish of his exile. In an attempt to prove

131

himself worthy of recall, he set himself to writing the two treatises just described.

But the hope of return to Florence was a deception, and in 1310, when the new Emperor Henry VII came down into Italy, filling the long-vacant chair as head of the empire and hoping to consolidate this part of his realm, Dante and other exiles saw in him the answer to their prayers. He had already in the *Convivio* described in Aristotelian terms the necessity for peace during which men could exercise virtue and the full use of the intellect. Peace of this sort could be attained only through the control of a supreme ruler devoid of personal ambitions whose aim is solely harmonious peace between cities and nations, down to the very wards of the cities. Universal empire or monarchy, indispensable to the well-being of mankind, he defined as the Roman Empire, brought into existence for this very purpose by God himself.

The supreme ruler he saw as Henry VII, and in a letter grave and joyful he addressed the princes and people of Italy, urging them to welcome him as the just restorer of peace to faction-ridden Italy. But Florence, like the other communes reluctant to yield up her hard-earned independence, became the center of opposition to Henry. At her opposition Dante erupted into rage and wrote an invective letter to the "most wicked Florentines within the city" threatening them with impending destruction, accusing them of opposition to the Lamb who was to remove the sins of the world. Within a month of this letter he wrote directly to Henry urging him to proceed directly against this leader of the opposition, this viper, this vixen, this corruption, Florence.

To the opposition of Florence was added that of Robert

of Naples, and then that of Clement V; when in 1313, toward the end of summer, Henry VII died on the plains of Buonconvento, Dante's hopes were blasted. It is probable that at this time he began the great defense of the principle of empire which goes under the title of *Monarchy*. His letter-writing had, no doubt, something to do with the renewal of the sentence of banishment against him in September, 1311, because at this time other exiles were allowed to return. But Dante's passionately held convictions, now crystallized and in the process of being incorporated into the treatise on monarchy, transcended both personal and civic interests for the larger philosophical and political concerns.

In scholastic terminology the treatise gives us a complete account of Dante's political theory: that universal empire is necessary to human welfare, that the Roman people have assumed empire by right, and that their authority comes directly from God. We have met this theory in small in the *Convivio*. The supreme ruler will respect the differing needs of the various nations, and obviously their differing needs will be cared for by the individual princes interpreting the imperial law. The third book of the treatise in particular provides us with a theory which we are to meet again in the *Divine Comedy:* the independence of temporal authority of the emperor from the authority of the papacy. The idea had been forcefully stated by Frederick II, and Dante adopts it anew, insisting that just as the moon derives only its light and not its existence from the sun, so the empire derives only spiritual grace, not its existence, from the papacy. Their functions as offices are different furthermore, being complementary and even interrelated. Man's nature being both mortal and immortal, his earthly goals—the pursuit of happiness and the acquisition of intellectual and moral virtue (in an Aristotelian sense)—are to be guaranteed by the temporal authority; his supernatural goals are the business of the spiritual authority. Each of them provides its own kinds of law to curb and guide man's fallen nature. Yet their relationship is not one of dependence upon each other but a harmonious recognition of the scope and compass of the other's authority.

The remainder of Dante's life was devoted principally to his great poem, perhaps the greatest monument of the age. After the battle of Montecatini in 1315, in a general amnesty granted by Florence, Dante could have come home to his beloved city upon admission of guilt. This Dante scornfully refused in a bitter letter, insisting that his innocence, his long labors in study, his status as a learned man, deserved much better. Florence in return passed sentence again, this time including Dante's sons in the charges.

In his last seven or eight years Dante seems to have found some measure of peace and personal security, mainly in Ravenna with Guido Novello, working away at the *Divine Comedy* and still nursing a hope that he would receive the laurel in Florence as a final acknowledgement of his genius. From Ravenna he engaged in an old-fashioned correspondence in Latin eclogues with Giovanni del Virgilio.

Giovanni reproaches him for writing in the vernacular, suggesting some subjects to be written in Latin. Dante replies with an affection touched by faint irony: when he has finished the *Paradiso* he confidently expects to be crowned with the laurel in Florence. Anyway he is sending a sample of ten cantos to convince Giovanni of their worth. In another pair of eclogues Giovanni invites Dante to come to receive the adulation he deserves in Bologna, and Dante writes a gentle refusal. Even at the end of life, Dante obviously is continuing his study of the ancient poets and here presents his own refinement of the tradition. In this same period, in 1320, Dante wrote a treatise on the relative levels of water and land, a proof of his dedication to scientific matters. Within the next year, returning from an embassy to Venice on behalf of his benefactor, he contracted fever and died, on September 14, 1321.

He was buried by Guido with great honor in the church of St. Peter Major, later called St. Francis. Over the centuries the tomb was gradually brought to its present state. Florence after his death tried to restore Dante's bones to his native city, but Ravenna successfully resisted her attempts. In 1865, on the occasion of the sixth centenary of his birth, Florence erected a monument to him in Santa Croce, but a worthy monument yet remains to be created. It is unfortunate that Michelangelo, who offered to do a memorial worthy of the poet, never received the commission to do so. His real monument is Italy itself, which accepts him as its greatest poet in a heartfelt conviction that well accords with Dante's own most intimate convictions about the unity of the peninsula.

The Divine Comedy

When Dante first conceived the idea of his great poem we cannot be sure. We remember as early as 1290 the promise at the close of the *Vita Nuova* to say something of Beatrice, with the help of God, such as had never been said before. More important perhaps, we remember the increasing disillusion of the passing years in exile as Dante regarded the political chaos of the peninsula. The ideals of love, those of philosophy, could in no way prepare him for the disillusion of an Italy perennially at odds with itself and without any hope of permanent peace. His own experience at the hands of Boniface and the evolution of his theory with regard to universal monarchy, his hopes for satisfactory earthly goals as well as spiritual salvation, led somehow to a conflation of the promise to praise Beatrice with the vision of a world adrift of its moorings. The pattern he decided upon was the familiar one of a pilgrimage in which he himself, with tremendous subjectivity, would participate as the chief agent. He would unify through his own experience the fates of many whom he planned to encounter on his journey, making them all in turn aspects of a law of order and love.

The poem would be doctrinal, didactic as well as pleasurable, a warning to all readers of their role in the general perversion of the times. Being Christian it would depict the various realms within Hell, Purgatory, and Paradise; and its pilgrim Dante would be shown as having wandered from the straight path and as being brought back gradually to a clear recognition of his goal *in patriam*. It would be, according to the concept of the time, a comedy; that is to say, it would contain some elements of the low style; it would begin in sadness, but it would have a happy ending. It would be written in keeping with the poet's conviction that poetry worthy of the name should have a significance beyond the mere surface events, meanings bearing upon various aspects of man's political, moral, and spiritual obligations.

Such may have been the conception of the poem, a flowering in the midst of adversity, which now took precedence over the interests of the other treatises in process in the first decade of the fourteenth century. Their concerns and subject matter are important, to be sure, but in no way are they to be compared to the great revelation which came to him to provide a vision of the highest ideals both in civic and in religious life, combining in himself so to speak the missionary zeal of Aeneas in the founding of Rome and that of St. Paul in the propagation of the faith.

What the individual stages of composition were, what changes in conception occurred during the composition, at what place or pace ideas crystallized we cannot really know. The style grows more controlled, some think, as the poem progresses. There is a greater consciousness of art; the diction becomes perfectly attuned to the subject matter. Number controls the structural details. After the necessary tripartite division three appears as the basis of the tercet which is the basic block of the canto; there are thirty-three cantos to each canticle, with an introductory canto adding up to an even one hundred. These cantos contain on each level of the otherworldly experience nine realms plus one other to make up the number ten. Even the moral system is based upon the triad of incontinence, violence, and fraud or malice in Hell; distorted, insufficient, and excessive love in Purgatory; and secular, active, and contemplative lives in Paradise. When we further consider that Dante strives throughout to keep the cantos close to each other in number of lines, that he employs various devices for symmetry and balance, that the word "stars" appears as the last word of each canticle, that the great discussion of love occupies the very center of the poem, we realize that nothing is casual in the art of this greater writer. Indeed the greater our conversance with the poem, the greater our admiration for a mind which demonstrates an infinite capacity for detail.

The poem is a marvel of structure, but most awesome is the thematic coherence of its moral, political, and spiritual meanings. Containing as it does the reflections of Dante's tremendous knowledge of politics and history, science and theology, the work tempts students into reading it from particular points of view. But the work is a poem, not a tract or a treatise, however doctrinal its purpose; and the "science" it contains is subordinated to the larger meaning that comes into existence almost without our complete understanding. This is to say that the work is compact, organically unified. Although many readers do not get beyond the first third of the poem, and even here tend to see the successive cantos as a series of episodes, the whole meaning of the poem emerges only when we read it entirely as a continuous structure having, in Aristotelian terms, a beginning, a middle, and an end, and when we consider that it furthermore arouses in its audience the emotions appropriate to the type and successfully effects the catharsis of these emotions.

Dante's artistic views maintain that poetry must have a meaning beyond its mere surface. An elaboration of this notion was expressed in the *Convivio*. A further development of the idea is to be found in a well-known letter addressed to Can Grande, and offering some suggestions concerning ways in which to approach the poem. It has become the habit with some scholars to deny the authenticity of this epistle; nonetheless the whole tone and scholastic character of the letter, with its valuable insights into the informing principles of the poem, favor the ascription to Dante. In it, the older fourfold method of interpretation still exists, but in a somewhat more refined statement. The allegorical, the moral, and the anagogical levels may for convenience be seen collectively as the spiritual or "other" meaning of the poem which is implicit in the purely surface narrative. In keeping with this binary system, then, the subject of the

138

poem is twofold: on the literal level, a pilgrimage in which the protagonist witnesses the state of souls after death in the three realms of the other world: on the spiritual or allegorical level, the condition of this life in which man, by the use or abuse of his will, merits reward or punishment. The aim of the poem, then, is to use all of the means available to poetry to teach, and in teaching, to free the reader from the misery of a disordered moral, social, and political life, and to lead him, after present bliss, to the happiness of communion with God. The philosophy is moral, because the intention of the poem is practical. Its title, the *Comedy,* forecasts its happy ending, and its conviction is that man can, under the guidance of the temporal ruler, live in a peace which guarantees him leisure to use his intellect, and that under the guidance of a spiritual ruler, he may learn to order his disordered soul and thus attain union with God.

The plot can be simply stated: at the age of thirty-five, Dante finds himself in a dark wood. The year is 1300, and the time, Easter week. How he came here he cannot say. He attempts to climb a hill on whose top he can see the light of the sun, but he is prevented from doing so first by a leopard, gaily spotted, then by a raging lion, and finally by a hungry wolf. Abandoning his intention he returns to the valley below, where he is accosted by a spirit figure, Virgil, poet of the Roman Empire, and thought by the Middle Ages to be the prophet of Christ's coming; Virgil is to function as Dante's guide along another path, that is, through Hell and the larger part of Purgatory. Thereafter, Beatrice, responsible for sending Virgil to be his guide, will take him through the various ranges of Heaven until he may be vouchsafed the supreme vision. Such is the literal level.

139

On the other level—and we are necessarily superficial here—we have an extended metaphorical meaning. Dante is man at a crucial stage in life, in a state of intellectual and moral disorder. He attempts to find his way out of the confusion but cannot do so without assistance, the way out of misery being blocked by his dominant passions. With the aid of natural reason, man is able to accomplish the initial stages of his improvement, to look honestly at the sources of misery and unhappiness not only in himself but in the society of which he is a part and to which he contributes. He is able gradually to recognize the various guises of evil, acquiring in the process some measure of self-control; thereafter he learns to assume the full measure of responsibility both as an individual and as a social creature. The process involves the painful difficulties of relinquishing one's recalcitrance toward God, gradual awakening of love for Him, and willingness to make amends. The process, so difficult to undertake, becomes easier as the higher rungs are achieved, especially since the soul finds itself co-operating with Divine grace which draws the soul quite naturally toward its destined goal. Through the various stages of Revelation for which he becomes eligible, he sees through Beatrice's eyes the various ways in which the perfected soul may serve its Maker. The logical end of such service is full participation in the divine community, which means of course sharing in a purified way in the love between the Creator and creation. Only a glimpse of this perfected life of grace can be granted Everyman, who has acted for the reader as one in the process of salvation.

It is obvious that such a scheme, seen from this allegorical point of view, lends itself admirably to extending its meaning out of any merely moral level into an entirely political level, and that Dante intends those doctrines at which he had arrived first in the *Convivio* and then in the *Monarchia* to be taken at full value. We can see, too, how such a scheme could come to be at once a personal document as well as an encyclopedia, a summation of the intellectual, political, moral, and religious data of the time.

The reader who follows the whole process, who makes an effort to recover the necessary philosophical and historical data to make the various episodes real, who is willing to surrender himself to the power of the poem, to its intellectual compression and its bursts of passion, will sooner or later appreciate why Dante is for Italians and many others the very king of poets. After him would come many great in their own right, but without that comprehensive genius, that moral vision which from its vantage saw life whole and saw it clearly. The faintly condescending attitude of Petrarch to the poem which Boccaccio had laboriously copied and then sent him is in its way a judgment which subtly lowers the one and elevates the other in a curious paradox of history.

Boccaccio (1313–75)

By comparison with Dante and with his revered friend Petrarch, Boccaccio falls into the third place among the great writers of Tuscan literary history. But Boccaccio needs no apology. His contributions to the mainstream of literature and that of scholarship are very great; the *Decameron* alone, with its pungent realism and its caustic ironies, is enough to insure his fame in posterity forever.

Looking back upon his youth as he was entering upon old age, Boccaccio wrote: ". . . I was disposed by nature for poetry from birth." His father, however, was bent upon educating him for a life of commerce and apprenticed him to a merchant, after the early study of arithmetic, for a period of six irrevocable years. Seeing that young Giovanni was not apt for business, his father put him to the study of canon law for another period of almost six years. But even under the guidance of a famous teacher, he rejected the discipline, the parental pressure, and the recriminations of his friends for that other life as poet.

Attaining his majority, he turned wholly to the pursuit of a career in literature. Long after he was a successful writer he lamented that, had his father but guided him into the sympathetic discipline of literature, he would now be truly ranked among the great poets.

The lost years were not a total waste. The stuff of life to which he was exposed in these early years was to show up on virtually every page he wrote. For up until the great bank failures of 1340 when his father summoned him home to Florence, his intellectual and emotional life was being shaped by the years of residence in Naples where ostensibly he was studying canon law. And through his friendship with the wealthy Niccolò Acciaiuoli, he was introduced to court life under King Robert.

Two influences there were to govern his thinking all his life. The first was his famous love affair with Maria d'Aquino, the Fiammetta who appears in one guise or another in the romances he wrote. The second was his exposure to scholarship under the guidance of Andalò di Negro, the astronomer, of Paul of Perugia, the compiler of myths, and of Barlaam, the Calabrian monk who introduced both Boccaccio and later Petrarch in 1342 to the elements of Greek. One interest sustains him as a creative poet; the other as compiler and scholar.

Under the influence of his love for Maria there poured

forth a succession of romances in prose and verse, some written in Naples, others in Tuscany. Whether he writes in the flush of love or in the bitterness of disillusion, the romances demonstrate the uses of experience. As Fiammetta, Maria is the motive behind most of the long tales and poems written during the Neapolitan sojourn and the decade that followed. The story of Florio and Biancofiore he rendered from ottava rima into prose at her behest, under the title *Filocolo*. Boccaccio serves an apprenticeship here in the language of the passions and sharpens his eye for landscape and setting.

The next two poems, the *Filostrato* (1338?) and the *Teseida* (1339–40), show the poet still following his muse, but by this time he and Maria have quarreled, and the breach between them has become irremediable. "You have gone to Samnium," he writes in the dedication of the *Filostrato,* "and I have searched, in old stories, for a person to serve as a messenger of my secret and wretched love. Such a person I have found in Troilus, Priam's son, who loved Criseyde. His woes are my story." The tale he tells, then, is familiar to students of Chaucer as the basis of *Troilus and Criseyde*.

What is new and purely Boccaccian is the minutely detailed psychology of the joy of love and the dolors of rejection and betrayal. The plot is carefully worked out, its inner pathos heightened by creating in the character of Criseyde a sensual woman of the world, for the most part a realist without excessive self-recrimination, and in the character of Troilus, an irresolute and callow youth who is as much the victim of his romantic personality as of fate. As the go-between, a common figure in romance, Boccaccio has created the ambiguous figure of Pandarus, and bequeathed an ugly name to posterity. Pandarus is largely responsible

143

for the details of bringing the lovers to the consummation of their love affair, and later scholarship has been divided between those who see him as a thoroughly depraved lecher and those who see him as a somewhat realistic friend. In the Boccaccian version its heightened passion, its sensual characters contribute to a somewhat damaging, if honest, picture of Neapolitan society.

Artistically the poem marks the introduction of ottava rima as a vehicle for poetry, and the development of a language adequate to express great psychological range. These advances in technique Boccaccio incorporates into the second of his "epic" poems, the *Teseida*. Here Boccaccio is writing of the three great subjects of romance: love, war, and virtue. Like the *Aeneid* it is written in twelve books and contains the same number of lines. It is, furthermore, under the same autobiographical influence as the previous poem, Fiammetta being intended to see in one of the agents the plight and suit of Boccaccio himself. Yet, we note, the self-conscious statement of his frustrations has begun to give way to the more exacting demands of his art.

More interesting than its opening episodes of war between Theseus of Athens and the Amazons and then between Theseus and Creon of Thebes is the love of Palamon and Arcita for Emily, sister of the queen. It is in the depiction of love, anguish, and jealousy that Boccaccio is deeply moving. Chaucer recognized the degree to which a purely human interest resided in this aspect of the romance. In his own adaptation he relegated the epic parts to the level of a frame and placed the emphasis on the central debate of love. Subsequent to Chaucer the tale received treatment by Shakespeare and Fletcher in *The Two Noble Kinsmen,* and later by Dryden in *Palamon and Arcite,* proof over the centuries of Boccaccio's gift for plots. Like the *Filostrato,* the *Teseida* represents a stage in the artist's development in which we see the poet still grappling with the problem of suitable diction, while widening the scope of the literary type. The elevations of tragic romance are not so high as to prevent our seeing that the situation, for all its panoply of tournaments and temples, is close to human experience.

In the *Ameto,* a pastoral allegory written in a mixture of prose and verse somewhat like the *Vita Nuova* of Dante, the personal element is still describable, particularly in the cry of longing for the courts of Naples, now that he is home in Florence. This is restricted, however, to a few verses at the very end of the poem in which he contrasts the two cities: Naples, a place of grace, pleasure, and love; Florence, a place of sadness and melancholy; the house in which he is to live, dark, silent, holding him against his will to his uncouth father.

The tale itself of a rough shepherd who falls in love with the nymph Lia traces out what may be thought to be a central concept in the Boccaccian ethos: the power of love to subdue the savage in human nature and to convert it to better social uses, a theme which stands also midway in the *Decameron* (v. 1). In the sprawling framework, Lia and six other nymphs represent the cardinal and theological virtues, and each enlists Ameto in the service of Venus. Philosophically the poem is a strange mixture of the sacred and the profane, of the antique and the modern. Clearly an experiment, it is also a groping for a new conviction about the role of love in human affairs, a facing up to the full range of human experience which would bear its full ripe fruit in the *Decameron.*

To the early forties belongs also the *Amorosa Visione,* a

poem in terza rima, in which visions of wisdom, fame, love, and wealth are vouchsafed to a lover. Led by a beautiful woman to a castle, he enters the gate of this world. Within, the visions are spread out as paintings worthy of Giotto's hand upon the walls: Dante serves as an illustration of wisdom, his own father as an example of avarice, and his beloved Maria as one of the lovers. Her he is enjoined to serve, and with her he walks into a grove talking of love. At the point at which he is about to embrace her, he wakes.

The poem reveals at every turn the influence of Dante, but the glorification of sensual passion and the deliberate turning away of the lover from the narrow gate of virtue toward the other gate of the rewards of this world is pure Boccaccio. Pure Boccaccio too is the acrostic formed by taking the first letters of the 1,500 tercets and forming with them two sonnets and a ballata dedicating the poem to "dear Fiamma, for whom my heart burns," and assuring her that the author who sends the vision to her is none other than Giovanni Boccaccio.

Of the remaining works of fiction, *Fiammetta,* a psychological novel in prose, and the *Ninfale Fiesolano,* a pastoral tale in ottava rima once more, are of their kind small masterpieces. The *Fiammetta* draws upon details from real life, but inverts the relationships of Fiammetta and her lover: the lover, called back to Florence by his aged father, abandons his sweetheart for another love. Is Giovanni having a belated revenge upon Maria? Whatever the case, Boccaccio is still mining an old experience while gravitating toward what he knew best, the irony of life itself. Here it is clear that Boccaccio has a firm grasp upon the psychology of thwarted love. The *Filostrato* afforded an exercise in male complaint, but now he pours out the grievances of betrayed

Fiammetta with an uncannily apt knowledge of the tormented female soul in the grip of an insuperable passion.

The *Ninfale Fiesolano* is a success on entirely different grounds. In it the groping poet now emerges into a serenity of outlook, a control of fresh and unpretentious diction which crowns the years of his apprenticeship. Its tragic story of the love of the shepherd Africo for the nymph Mensola, a virgin dedicated to chaste Diana, is intended in Ovidian style to relate the origin of two streams which flow down from Fiesole into the Arno. Their guilty love, the suicide of Africo, the birth of a child, and the conversion of Mensola into a stream are handled in a classically restrained manner, but with a special Boccaccian grasp of the human realities involved in the tragic story. At the close of the poem, the court of chaste nymphs of which Mensola had been a member is dissolved, and the nymphs are relegated to matrimony in a typical vote against asceticism. In it, in effect, the ascetic and otherworldly ideal of the Middle Ages is given a *coup de grâce,* and the realism of the later Renascence seems once and for all to absorb for its own uses the stuff of erotic life.

The earlier poems, romances, epics, pastorals, had gradually led him successfully to a style and flexible diction adequate for the next phase. Maturity had brought with it, too, the recognition of his natural instinct for realism, for ironical comedy, for ridicule. His facility with sentimental aspects of experience and powers of sharp observation enabled him to use the materials from all classes of life and to get at the essentially human. The tremendous range of powers tested in his earlier poems he brought to bear upon the *Decameron.* The occasion for the work is the Plague itself, and here Boccaccio distinguishes himself as a clinical observer and reporter of the ravages wrought in the city in 1348. With Villani he remains the surest source of our knowledge of the terror which struck the city.

The pestilence, once started, spread like fire; people shunned each other; groups formed, hoping that by temperate living they might escape infection; some ate only carefully selected foods, diverting their minds from fear with music and other entertainments. Others took their pleasures wildly. Property was neglected; the operations of law were neglected. Men did as they pleased. Many deserted the city for the country, "as if God . . . intended the destruction only of those remaining within the walls of the city."

Social and family life were rent apart by the mounting horrors, and in the general dearth of assistance, many died who might have lived; morality, modesty, and custom staggered under the burden of the more pressing demands of survival. The formal funeral rites, with entourage of mourners, procession to church, candles, and singing, were abandoned, the sick dying unattended. The bodies were dragged out and deposited at the door to be picked up by porters for burial. Indifference became the defense against too much horror and fear. Upwards of one hundred thousand persons died between March and July.

Amidst the horrors, seven young ladies—so runs Boccaccio's opening—assemble in Santa Maria Novella to discuss the general dissolution of moral life in the ravaged city. They decide to go to the country to escape the stench of disease, taking with them three young men to act as escorts. In the morning they make their way to a villa about two miles out of Florence, and there they plan their holiday. Each day's activities will be governed by one of the young people in turn. In order to while away the warm hours of the afternoon each person will tell a story for the entertainment of the others. Each day's tales will be governed by a leader, whose task is to set the theme: tales of happiness, of adventure, of trickery, of wit, of sorrow, and much more.

The range of the tales is so tremendous as to enable us to place Boccaccio in inventiveness of character and situation with the great raconteurs of any age. A range from the most banal to the most serious emotions invests the collection with a pervasive interest. Men and women of all varieties parade before us in a controlled balance of style and intellectual exuberance. Romance, tragedy, pathos, comedy, realism, and bitter irony all come within the scope of this masterpiece.

Some tales are more vivid than others. The comic pieces have tended to repress our memory of the more romantic tales, but it is a mistake to see only the base aspects of experience as the chief representatives of the *Decameron*. It contains pungently told tales that have nothing to do with boudoir intrigue, heroes and heroines of great emotional depth and nobility, tales of deeply appealing sweetness of sentiment. They are, for reasons of human nature, not as popular as some others, but they are there. The splendid defense of friendship in the story of Titus and Gisippus, the grand vindication of magnanimity in the tale of Nathan, and the rare denial of self in the tale of Griselda (the tale moral Petrarch singled out for translation into Latin) enable us to see how Boccaccio, later in his life, could justify poetry as an instrument for teaching, like theology.

One cannot say, however, that the dominant effect of the *Decameron* is moral. Its tone is that of a quiet and detached irony at the spectacle of mankind in the grip of passions. Indignation and bitter satire, even in the tales of wanton clerics, are dissipated in a rather genial acceptance of human nature. The law of life for all is love stripped of any Dantean, transcendental character. It becomes a destinal force which the learned can accommodate or resign themselves to, and which the ignorant blindly obey. It is this quality of life seen without idealism, without shirking the conviction of an erotic basis for all sentimental experience, which more than the naughtiness of the tales freezes the moral critic. Like Chaucer, Shakespeare, and Rabelais, Boccaccio's vision embraces the world. It does not shrink from its trickery and deceit, its appetite-driven souls. The comprehensive humanity of the writer focuses our attention upon the world as interesting in itself, without reference to the spiritual world. *Caveat lector!*

Boccaccio knew that literature has the power to persuade; twenty years later, after a spiritual crisis and the friendship with Petrarch, Boccaccio expressed his opinion of the *Decameron* in an altered tone of voice. He begged his friend Mainardo Cavalcanti not to allow the women of his house to read these "trifles" on the ground that there is much in them that is less than decent, much that can arouse the passions. I was young, he pleads, and commanded to do it by one in authority.

These twenty years were years in which much happened to change the course of his career and interests. Although he had achieved reputation and prestige, he was poor. Over the period from 1350 to 1367 he was engaged in a number of civil tasks, some of which no doubt helped him eke out his livelihood. Two are of special interest here: in 1350, Florence sent him to Ravenna to make a gift of ten gold florins to Sister Beatrice, Dante's daughter, at that time a nun in the convent of Santo Stefano dell' Uliva. And in

1351 he was given the pleasant responsibility of conveying to Petrarch at Padua, Florence's offer of a restored citizenship, the restitution of his father's property, and a professorship at the Florentine University. Although Petrarch did not accept the offer, it was for Boccaccio an especially happy visit with the man whom he had known personally for less than a year, but whom he had admired for a long time. (He had entertained Petrarch in Florence in 1350 when that poet was on his way to Rome for the Jubilee.)

The association with Petrarch was, as a matter of fact, a new spring for Boccaccio. Their relationship became somewhat that of master and disciple. Boccaccio was ripe for the new direction into which Petrarch diverted his intellectual energies. However, one last effort in autobiographical fiction, quite apart from Petrarch's influence, appeared in 1354–55. The *Corbaccio* is a disaffected attack upon women, malicious and personal in tone, and unlike the more genial and detached voice heard in the *Decameron,* a far cry from the usual disposition of a Boccaccio so equitable of temper as to be called *Johannes tranquillitatum,* or as his own disciple Benvenuto da Imola called him, *placidissimus.* The fountains of poetic energy have gone brackish. In the association with Petrarch over almost twenty-five years of his life, his intellectual energies are henceforth put mainly to the service of learning.

From his hand there came now a succession of Latin works: a collection of Bucolics (1351–66); nine books of the *Falls of Illustrious Men* (1355–60) which did much to crystallize a pattern for the tragedy on the Continent; a similar treatise *On Famous Women;* the great compilation of myths drawn from various sources under the title *The Genealogy of the Gentile Gods,* to which he appends a vig-

151

orous defense of poetry, published in the 1370's; a geographical dictionary describing places named in classical literature. Somewhat jejune by later standards, they established his reputation as a Latin scholar and compilator. Boccaccio's first biographer, Filippo Villani, praises him not for the *Decameron* but for these Latin writings.

Vastly more to the credit of both Boccaccio and Petrarch, perhaps, is their contribution to the revival of Greek studies in Italy, some of which we have sketched out elsewhere. In the early 1340's both men had been introduced to the study of Greek by the Calabrian monk Barlaam. By 1360, Boccaccio had come to know of Leon Pilatus, another Calabrian, already an acquaintance of Petrarch and at work on a partial translation of Homer into Latin for him. Perhaps on the suggestion of Petrarch, Boccaccio worked to bring Pilatus to Florence, where at great trouble to himself he arranged for a chair of Greek at the University. For well-nigh three years Boccaccio endured him in his own house, where Leon's vile manners and irascible temper must have been a severe trial. For the sake of the version of Homer which Petrarch had instigated, Boccaccio tolerated the uncouth man and took notes humbly from his volatile tongue. From this endurance contest Petrarch remained aloof in Padua, offering advice on the art of translation from afar.

The version which the two poets finally got was far from an accurate rendition, but for Boccaccio it was a door opened on the great past. Besides, Pilatus was a reservoir of interesting tales, myths, and tidbits of information which Boccaccio was to use to great advantage in the *Genealogy*. The association enabled him to say later with pride that his was the glory of having restored Greek poetry to Tuscany; that he was the first to bring to Florence, at his own expense,

Homer and "the other Greek poets"; and that he was the first to study, alone, the *Iliad,* with Leon. One admires here the zeal, the patience, the determination to widen his range.

This period of Boccaccio's life was, owing perhaps to the turmoil of the times and a persistent inner distrust, a time of spiritual crisis. In such a state of mind he received a message brought him from the deathbed of Blessed Peter Petroni, a Sienese Carthusian. The dying monk had had a vision of the world *sub specie aeternitatis,* with a glimpse into the future of some eminent men of his time, Boccaccio and Petrarch among them. Their deaths were at hand unless they abandoned profane literature. In a panic of indecision and hasty judgment, Boccaccio resolved to give up the life of study, to dissolve his library, to suppress his amorous poems and tales, and to give himself up to a life of prayer.

In such a state of mind he wrote to Petrarch, offering to sell his library to him. The answer he received is an ever-lasting monument to the sane humanity of the older man, a proof of the tremendous trust placed in him by the younger. Firmly, soundly, Petrarch argued against the terms of the vision and against hasty action of any sort. The letter's insistence that literature excites virtue in man's heart and serves also to diminish the fear of death, that it can be made to serve in the defense of religion, is part and parcel of Petrarch's own deep and special sort of religiosity. Its sincerity and calmness cleared the air for Boccaccio and cured him of the disease.

Their association continued throughout their lifetimes. After a galling trip to Naples at the invitation of Niccolò Acciaiuoli, his friend and patron, Boccaccio spent several months in Venice, in 1367. Petrarch was away in Pavia unfortunately, but Boccaccio describes with deep affection and profound emotion his reception by Petrarch's daughter and her husband. Most endearing is his account of greedily embracing their child Eletta. To Boccaccio she was like his own child—a mysterious chapter in his life—who had died. In Eletta he saw "the same face, expression, eyes, laughter, gestures, walk, carriage. . . . Alas, how often as I held your Eletta in my arms and listened to her chatter, did the thought of my own child taken from me bring tears to my eyes. These I let flow later, with much sighing, when no one could see them." The sentiment of the letter is of a piece with his fourteenth Eclogue in which he sees his daughter in the pleasant environs of Paradise.

The last years of Boccaccio's life, save for embassies and a trip to Naples in 1371, were spent in the refuge of Certaldo, away from the bitter animosities of Florentine life. Here, with delight, he could read in peace. But in 1373, when he was sixty, his long interest in and study of Dante earned for him a signal honor: Florence made Boccaccio the first public lecturer on the *Divine Comedy,* the lectures to be given at the church of Santo Stefano at the Badia. The commentary on the *Comedy* which may have been the stuff of his lectures is the last substantial work to come from his pen, and extends unfortunately only to the seventeenth canto, the seventeenth line of the *Inferno.*

But his health rapidly declined, and he was back in Certaldo in October of the next year. There he received the news of the death of his beloved Petrarch. Weak and tremulous, as he describes himself, with a face grown stupid with disease, he lingered on watching the seasons change over the hills until, on December 21, 1375, the grace of God, on which he had been waiting, released him from his life. His epitaph he had himself written:

The Three Crowns of Tuscany

Beneath this stone lie the bones and ashes of John.
His soul now stands before God, clad in the merit
Won in the toils of this mortal life. His father was
Boccaccio,
His native ground, Certaldo, his dedication and
study, divine poetry.

In his way, Boccaccio had been an innovator and a pioneer; in literary criticism as well as in poetry his name resounds down the corridors of the years. In Italy, Salutati, Sacchetti, Pulci, Tasso, Ariosto; in England, Chaucer, Shakespeare, Spenser, Keats, Tennyson, to name but a few, could find in him the sources of their own inspiration. Upon his death Sacchetti could lament with Salutati that the mansions of Parnassus were now empty. The first great age of Italian literature was over.

Petrarch (1304–74) and the New Learning

"Petrarch was," to borrow a line from his latest biographer Ernest Wilkins Hatch, "the most remarkable man of his time; and he is one of the most remarkable men of all time." It was the habit of an earlier generation of scholars to characterize him as the first modern man, the first modern scholar and man of letters, the first humanist, all of them terms of exaggeration, but a measure of the great fascination which Petrarch the poet, writer, thinker, and psychologist exerts upon our sensibilities. His life overlaps that of Dante, and for the last third of his life he and Boccaccio were close friends; they all shared a common love for Italy as a political entity, and they shared a common literary tradition, but their interpretation of the times and their uses of the past are distinctly their own. Dante in a sense sums up an era, which is a way of saying that he comes at the end of it, rooting his moral vision of it in the philosophical tradition of Aristotle and St. Thomas. Petrarch, less rigidly schematic, more introspective, more self-conscious, pushes aside scholasticism and the age that produced it in favor of the tradition of Plato and St. Augustine.

Many of his attitudes toward religion are thoroughly conventional; he thought much on the virtuous life and salvation, reproaching himself for an excessive love of this world. Politically, too, he is orthodox, clinging to the familiar notions of pope and emperor with their separate spheres of influence. But he is linked to the future securely by his achievement in lyric poems written to describe and to analyze his love for Laura, poems which in form and subjective emotional tone were to dominate the practice of later Continental poetry, and by his achievement as a scholar with the capacity to see in the literature of the past a perennially rewarding meaning applicable to the present. He can be credited not merely with discovering Cicero's *Familiar Letters* and Quintilian's *Institutes of Oratory,* but with editing and having copies made of ancient writings, and generously making them available to others.

In him then we see the beginnings, the seeds of the succeeding century, drawing to him by his ideas groups of learned men who in their turn explored much that his passion for knowledge had opened up. His devotion to the classics, his passionate search for manuscripts, his letters, and his poems all reveal aspects of a mind avid for the new. Speaking freely on a great variety of subjects, he reveals his own inner convictions on love and earthly glory, openly avowing for the latter that the world's great deeds are precisely the result of such a goal. When in April, 1341, he received the poet's crown in Rome he hailed it as the happiest, the most solemn day of his life, but, he adds, "not so much on my own account, as an incitement to others to attain excellence."

By inclination and conviction, Petrarch was a Platonist. This curious fact is explicable if we remember that Neo-Platonism had steadily filtered into Western thought, largely through the early doctrines of the church. Writers like his beloved Cicero, the pseudo-Dionysius, St. Augustine, and Boethius perpetuated for subsequent ages much of the Platonic burden which reappeared from time to time in various guises among Arab scholars, at Chartres, and in the *Romance of the Rose*. Even St. Thomas must pay more than passing attention to the writings and ideas of the Platonic tradition.

Yet Petrarch did not really know Greek. What the Middle Ages knew in general of Greek literature was in Latin translations, and for Plato this was principally the *Timaeus* in the Latin version of Chalcidius (fourth century). This Petrarch had, and possibly the *Meno* and *Phaedo*. His interest in Greek was keen enough, however, for him to seek instruction from the Calabrian monk Barlaam, who began to teach him fundamentals. This in itself is noteworthy, since he is the first humanist to start again that greatest of pagan traditions.

Petrarch's study of Greek, begun in 1342, was to have culminated in his reading Homer; but when Barlaam went on, through Petrarch's intercession, to become Bishop of Geraci in Calabria this hope was frustrated. In 1348, however, Petrarch met Nicholas Sygeros, from Constantinople, and from their conversations about Homer there resulted in 1354 the gift by Sygeros of the Greek texts of both poems of Homer. His letter of thanks to Sygeros complains that he longs to learn the language so that the poem which lies dumb before him will yield up its meaning. Five years later, in Padua, Petrarch was introduced to Leon Pilatus, and still impelled by his hope of translating the Great Greek, discussed him with Boccaccio in Milan and brought them together. Within the year, Pilatus was in Florence, occupying a chair of Greek at the University there, arranged by the goodhearted Boccaccio.

To Petrarch, Pilatus was a great monster, uncouth, ill-bred, ugly. To Boccaccio however, he presented a rare opportunity, and he entertained Pilatus in his home in the hope of bringing about a complete translation of Homer. Petrarch watched from afar, but his interest remained high, for he gave all kinds of advice, particularly that of St. Jerome on avoiding a literal translation. "Go on," he writes, "Give us back Homer who was lost to us." Eventually, by 1364 or 1365, the Pilatus version, largely supported by Boccaccio, was complete and parts of it in Petrarch's hands. "Penelope," he writes, "had not more ardently longed for Ulysses."

His love of Greek learning, however, kept him collecting the works of Plato, and at his death he had sixteen or so of his works, a tribute not only to the philosopher but to the indefatigable spirit of the scholarly Petrarch. His knowledge of the tradition, however, was drawn principally from Cicero and St. Augustine, and the emphasis he drew from them was mainly that of the virtuous life taught by philosophy. Following closely upon St. Augustine in his belief in the necessity of self-knowledge and the freedom of moral choice, his accent falls heavily on the great potential within the human agent acting here, in and for himself. While this does not deny the operations of grace, it does place in relief a belief in self-sufficiency which the next age was to blow up into a full-fledged self-confidence.

It is no wonder that Petrarch is called the first modern man. What makes him modern in his interest in the complexities of human nature, indeed in the complexities of his *own* human nature, and this more than his intense patriotism, more than his antiquarian studies, assures his reputation with posterity. Despising the medieval disciplines of theology, scholasticism, and jurisprudence, he turned with restless sensitivity to poetry as the all-transcending, all-encompassing art. His intellectual range is tremendous: as lyricist, epic poet, moralist, historian, polemicist, writer of essays and the familiar letter, he opened up the avenues the next age would pursue. If to the small sonnet form we add bucolic allegory and elegy, and to history we add biography, we can see, from the point of view of literature, the vastness of his contribution to his successors.

We add here what everyone notes in reading Petrarch—a feeling for the picturesque and a passion for describing landscape in great detail. In Petrarch it is deliberate and self-conscious, an attempt to reconstruct before the mind's eye what pleased his aesthetic soul. This accuracy of reportage goes hand in hand with an extreme realism in depicting human beings so as to make them appear vividly before our mind's eye—Robert of Hungary he describes as "short, bald, redfaced, with swollen legs, rotten with vice, leaning on a staff, bent over from hypocrisy, not disease."

The great poet cannot really be claimed by Florence. His father was exiled in the banishment of 1302, and Francesco was born in Arezzo, two years later. His subsequent life shows how little any city may claim him: a childhood in Avignon; a student's training at Montpellier and Bologna;

159

visits in his twenties to Paris, France, Flanders, Germany; Rome in his thirties; and more and more, toward the end of his life, Padua. Florence does not figure very much in his thinking, and he prefers the wider citizenship of Latium, of Rome, to that of his parents.

Florence, in 1349, having finally received from Clement VI full privileges to establish its University (efforts to found the *studium* had been going on since 1321), began to compete for renowned teachers in the various faculties. The new school secured immediately the services of a famed teacher of jurisprudence, Thomas Corsini. In 1351 it sought the services of Petrarch. Boccaccio was sent bearing a fulsome letter of invitation which sought to obliterate the shame of his father's exile a half-century earlier. In classical terms, it suggested that although the city had not had up to this time a program of liberal studies, plans now called for a full flowering of humanism so that Florence, like Rome, would surpass the other cities of Italy. Petrarch's letter of appreciation, wishing well to the Florentine Commune, is an evasive refusal. One can only speculate on what the University might have become with his presence.

Yet his influence burgeoned throughout Florentine intellectual circles; we may see in him the impetus for the cultural groups of the late fourteenth century. Two Florentines, one in the religious life, Friar Luigi Marsigli (1330?–94) of the Augustinian church Santo Spirito, and Coluccio Salutati (1330–1406), notary and chancellor of the Florentine Republic for a quarter of a century, both gathered around them groups of people interested in learned discussion.

When Marsigli was but a boy, he had been presented to Petrarch. The poet, favorably impressed by the lad's manners and deportment, predicted a fine career for him. Some twenty-five years later, in 1366, when Marsigli came to Padua to study theology, Petrarch urged him not to neglect literature, a field of knowledge necessary to the theologian. In 1373, the last year of his life, Petrarch sent to his dear friend his personal copy of the *Confessions* of St. Augustine, a book he had owned and studied for almost half a century. It had been, he tells us in a letter of great sweetness, his constant companion in travels, veritably a part of him. From Marsigli's hand has come down a commentary on *canzoni* by Petrarch, the fruit perhaps of their conversations together.

In Marsigli's hands the Petrarchan ideal of a theology supported by wide-ranging knowledge and a happy confluence between sacred and profane studies flourished. Into his cell in the monastery came his disciples, young and old, to discuss questions in moral philosophy and theology, and to be introduced to the study of antiquity. Coluccio himself was a steady attendant at the meetings, preparing his own part in the discussion beforehand, or thinking over what he would say, as he walked from his home to the convent. There, as we read in the records of the next century, the hours went by unnoticed as the learned Friar dazzled the company with his wide range of knowledge.

Speaking to Leonardo Bruni and to Niccolò Niccoli in 1401, Salutati says: "I know that you remember the theologian Luigi, a man of keen intelligence and remarkable eloquence, who has now been dead for seven years. . . . I used to go to his meetings frequently while he was alive. . . . Oh immortal Gods, how much rhetorical skill, how much information, what a memory he had! Not only did he have a grasp of religious matters, but also of what we call pagan subjects. He always had on his lips Cicero, Virgil, Seneca, and other ancients, and not merely their general views, but their very words. . . . I heard and learned much from him, and much about which I was in doubt, I confirmed on the authority of that man."

Much of this evidence, drawn from a dialogue of Leonardo Bruni (1369–1444), is further supported by that of Poggio Bracciolini (1380–1459), confirming information that the most outstanding men of Florence frequented Friar Marsigli's little academy, seeking out the learned man as a master and an oracle. These were, for the most part, men of maturity, and many of them contemporaries of the Augustinian. But some of them were the new and eager generation, Niccolò Niccoli, Giovanni di Lorenzo, Roberto Rossi, who passed from his influence as learned men, instructed in the best precepts of living. That his teaching was effective we may judge from at least one sonnet of the time which reproaches him for bringing the new knowledge to the tender minds of the young, and from a letter written by the commune to the general of the order to put an end to his teaching in Florence.

It is unfortunate that we do not have more information on Marsigli from his own time other than a few letters and his commentaries on Petrarch. Salutati, in one of his own letters, laments that he bequeaths no major writing to posterity, but, he adds, neither did Pythagoras, Socrates, or Christ. The records on which we rely, the *Dialogi ad Petrum Paulum Histrum* of Bruni, and the *Paradiso degli Alberti* by Giovanni da Prato, are of the early fifteenth century. The *Paradiso,* in which Marsigli is given much that is politically and historically exciting to say, while we may regard it with the suspicion which its literary genre necessitates,

yet serves to indicate how culture and learning of the So-
cratic kind—with dialogue and debate—had very early
diffused itself among the laity. It would be some time before
the Platonic Academy would come into existence, but in
the *Paradiso* we catch more than a glimmer of its method
and of its substance. Marsigli, once enjoined by Petrarch
personally in Padua to develop his philosophical strength
for the battle against unbelief, thus bore rich fruit in a succession of students who formed an intellectual bridge to the
coming age.

The practical man of the world, Coluccio Salutati, was
also the faithful student and scholar of Petrarch's lineage,
following the master in the collection of codices, even col-
lating texts and making lists of variants in a method which
the fifteenth century would employ. His home, too, was one
of those intellectual centers to which budding statesmen as
well as established citizens from the upper classes came to
listen and to learn.

His early training had been in law and in the discipline
of the notary, and the bulk of his career was in public office.
In 1367 he was chancellor of Todi; and in 1371, of Lucca;
and from 1375 until the end of his life, of the Florentine
Commune, presiding by both moral force and practical
action over the tumultuous political life of the last quarter
of the century. During this period he poured out a succession of treatises, orations, and Latin letters which are a
testament to an elevated spirit. Eloquence, in the sense of
rhetoric as the handmaid of the political life, in him enjoyed a resurgence. The letters, which reflect both his intense patriotism and his sense of a continuous Latin tradition, are largely free of that "official" frigid style of high
office. His letters are literary works, although they are also

163

diplomatic documents. So powerful were they that a Galeazzo Visconti professed himself to be more fearful of one of
his letters than of a thousand Florentine knights, and during
altercations with the Pope, they roused to revolt, by sheer
eloquence, territories belonging to the church.

As a humanist Salutati's reputation rests not merely upon
his epistolary style, his restoration of eloquence to style, nor
upon his philological endeavors—Poggio Bracciolini says
that he had 800 codices in his library—but upon the
thought to which Petrarch inspired him. In both the treatises
and the letters we may see the caliber of the man.

Like Petrarch, Salutati saw Platonism as a corroborator
of and a support for the good Christian life, its finest in-
gredient being its moral or ethical implications. The acquisition of virtue, in his view, was the victory over the self. The
questions which he discusses, like fate and free will, the
divinity inherent in nature, the good life, the control of the
passions, the relation between the active and the spiritual
life, the function of love in society, absolute Law, cycles in
history—all are subjects dear to the moral Platonist's heart
and open up that avenue to the later Renascence which
Petrarch had mapped out.

Bruni, who succeeded Salutati as chancellor, says in one
of his letters that he owed to Salutati his own knowledge of
Latin and Greek. As a matter of fact, Salutati, at the age
of sixty-five, was instrumental in bringing about a matter
crucial to the revival of ancient culture: the hiring of Manuel
Chrysoloras to teach Greek in Florence. In 1394–95, Chrysoloras had come on embassy to Venice from Constantinople
to seek assistance for his nation against the Turks, and
Coluccio had sent Roberto Rossi and Iacopo d'Angelo to
hear him lecture. On the basis of the reports, the commune,

on March 28, 1396, invited him to become professor of Greek at a starting salary of 100 gold florins. In early 1397, Chrysoloras came to Florence, and for three years, until 1400, expounded Greek language and literature to a succession of great students, continuing the labors of Boccaccio and Petrarch to open the door upon the greatness of the past. Much of the expense of the venture was borne by Palla Strozzi, then only in his middle twenties, who, according to his biographer Vespasiano da Bisticci, was anxious to bring the teacher to Florence and so sent to Greece for a great number of volumes at his own expense, including Ptolemy, Plutarch's *Lives,* the *Dialogues* of Plato, the *Politics* of Aristotle, and many others.

Chrysoloras' teaching of Greek was matched in Florence by the teaching of Latin by Giovanni Malpaghini, soon also to be lecturer on Dante in the chair established by Boccaccio. Even here Petrarch's pervasive influence is visible a quarter-century after his death, since Giovanni had been a favored protégé and scribe of the great poet from 1364 to 1368.

No account of Salutati would be complete without reference to the view of poetry which he shared with Boccaccio and Petrarch, in defense of which he wrote polemical letters and treatises. Recalling that the fathers of the church themselves dip generously into Virgil, he reminds his adversaries that the substance of poetry is a species of truth divinely ordained. But the fables of poetry are not to be accepted literally. Rather they are to be pierced by the eye of the mind to the inner core. The Sacred Scriptures themselves are species of poetry containing many tales, which, if accepted literally, would imperil the soul; to cast off the ancient world of poetry would be, in effect, to lose the sources of our knowledge of style, of diction, of literary grace. Salutati was especially attacked for these views by Blessed John Dominici at the beginning of the fifteenth century, and to him Coluccio was in the process of responding when death overtook him.

† † †

Intellectually these Florentines are standing at the gateway to a second Renascence. Petrarch cries out in one place that he stands on the borderline between the past and the future, that he speaks to coming generations, but we remember that he was peculiarly equipped to live simultaneously in the old world of revealed truth and in the new one of skeptical, private judgment. For better or for worse he had, by seeing himself at one with the ancients, opened Pandora's box, focusing the glance of posterity upon what is perennially human and ushering in an age which has not yet passed away.

8. The Recorders of History

BETWEEN THEM, Dino Compagni and the trilogy of Giovanni, Matteo, and Filippo Villani divide the century; and of the trio, Giovanni is by far the most interesting and even least biased. Dino describes the collapse and defeat of the White faction of the Guelf party; Giovanni and his followers recount the triumph of the Blacks. There are, to be sure, other historians of the period, particularly Marchionne di Coppo Stefani and Simone della Tosa, but no others have either the excitement of Dino or the reportorial skill of Giovanni, and to these two we will restrict our attentions.

Dino Compagni, of substantial merchant stock, was born in 1255? and died in 1324. His chief monument covers the crucial incidents not only of Dante's political career but of Florence's stormy day-to-day history within a restricted period ending in 1312. An active participant in civil affairs, he was a member of the silk guild in 1280, was one of its governing consuls six times between 1282 and 1299, and was a member of the group that established the priorate as the city's administration in 1282. He was the friend of Giano della Bella's reform of the early 1290's, was himself prior in 1289 and 1301, and Gonfalonier of Justice in 1293.

Not only was he a man of action in trade and politics but in literature and religious life as well. His name is grouped with that of Cino da Pistoia, Guido Cavalcanti, and Dante by a contemporary; a few sonnets have come down to us, work of not great merit, along with a *canzone* on the virtue to be sought by various estates, classes, professions; his name is associated with a longish allegory called *L'Intelligenza* which is of some interest. In the works of charity and mercy, Dino was a member of the Company of Mary of Orsanmichele, which alleviated the sufferings of the poor, serving as captain of the group in 1298.

His political career came to an end with the collapse of the White faction in 1301 because of his own antagonism to the Blacks and to the aims of Pope Boniface. As a White, he might have suffered exile under the victorious Blacks, but he was able to claim immunity under the law which prevents legal action against a prior within a year after his incumbency. Escaping exile and loss of property, he yet was finished as a politician; whereas his vote and voice were frequent in the various councils of the city up to that time, after 1301 he seems to disappear from the scene, living the life of a merchant and family man in his house overlooking the Arno.

His name might have dwindled into oblivion had he not sometime around 1310 begun to take hope with Dante that through the intercession of Henry VII, Florence might be disciplined under the imperial heel; and he began secretly to record his memories of the vicissitudes through which he had lived, in the fierce animosities of Guelfs and Ghibellines and of the two factions of the Guelf party. The *Chronicle* which he left to posterity has been vindicated by subsequent researches. Today there is no doubt that for its limited period it is the most dependable document of its kind. So authentic is it as history, and yet so personal, that Dino's name deserves to stand with that of other great names of his age, with that of Arnolfo, of Giotto, of Dante himself.

The story he tells is not a pretty one. Spanning the years from 1270 to 1312, it contains a central episode dealing with the collapse of the Whites through cowardice and general ineptitude in the fall of 1301, and with their attempts to return to power during the two successive years. We have dealt with this incident in the opening chapter, but we may recall here that the Blacks and the Whites, under the guidance respectively of the Donati and the Cerchi, were vying for control of the city. The Blacks, in league with Pope Boniface VIII, had conspired to bring into the city a peacemaker, Charles of Valois, who would really come to restore power to the Blacks. The agents in the terrible catastrophe in which Dino participates, like Corso Donati and Vieri de' Cerchi, are drawn with consummate skill.

Dino's attitude, though recorded sometime after the events in which he had participated, is passionate, and with Dante he shares the trait of high indignation coupled with grim prophecy. At the beginning of his account of the events of 1301, at that point at which he prepares to tell us of the arrangement to bring Charles into Florence as peacemaker, he cannot resist an outburst fraught with the terrible irony of hindsight: "Arise, O wicked citizens, full of discord, take up sword and fire, spread evil about. Reveal your wicked desires and terrible purposes. Don't delay, go and lay waste the beauties of your city. Shed the blood of your brothers, divest yourselves of faith and love, deny each other help and service. Tell your lies. . . . Do you think that God's justice has grown less? . . . Don't delay, wretches, for more is destroyed by one day of war, than can be gained by many years of peace. And small is that spark which brings a great kingdom to ruin."

The point of view expressed is not merely political but,

as in Dante, moral, ethical, religious; and it is embellished with outbursts like the terrible roll call of traitors and weaklings who let the city come to destruction, the lamentation over the destruction of Pistoia in 1306, and the proclamation with which he closes his account, predicting that the unrighteous citizen who have corrupted Florence will find themselves scourged by Emperor Henry VII—a familiar strain, but a hope blasted in the inexorable course of time by the death of the emperor.

Dino was not blind to the defects of his faction; their vacillation, their weaknesses are all laid out before us, and in damning his fellows inadvertently he damns himself. Their fault of being so hopeful of peace that they were easily deceived may in some measure attach to Dino. He has his moments of self-knowledge; he tells us how he wept many bitter tears over the indecision of the Whites who wished for peace when they should have been barricading themselves behind doors and sharpening weapons.

Death and the passage of time provide Dino with revenge upon the enemies of Florence. Boniface died mad at Rome in 1303, having been subjected to mental and physical outrage by the soldiers of Sciarra Colonna. The haughty, wily Corso, arrogant to the end, rode roughshod over his enemies, trying by one means or another to gain the upper hand in the city. In the final months of 1308 his last attempt in the city was foiled; crippled with gout and unable to bear arms, he stayed in the final fray which erupted in the piazza of San Pier Maggiore; "with his tongue he encouraged his friends, praising and cheering those who bore themselves valiantly." Finally beaten, he fled through the east gate of the city. There, on the way to the abbey of San Salvi, he was overtaken and pierced in the throat by a hired mercenary. Monks carried him into the abbey to die, the victim finally of those he had estranged.

On purely artistic grounds this little *Chronicle* is a masterpiece, not because of organization or skill in presentation but in the sheer energy which bursts through its economical wordage, and in the control to which he subjects his passionate indignation. Its portraits are unforgettable, the insights into human motives honest, the integrity of its point of view morally stirring. What is eloquent in Dino flows from his passionate sense of offended moral sentiment, as De Sanctis has suggested. His convictions leads him to pour out his judgments in hectic fashion. But the justifications, the condemnations, are recalled ten years after their occurrence. And the passage of time, while it has not healed all the wounds, has provided the distancing perspectives of moral commitment. While history demonstrates his errors, the moral order justifies the actions of the just. It is a point of view that only the greatest minds can carry off.

Alongside the passionate involvement and the somewhat wistful vindications of Dino, the more pedestrian chronicle of Giovanni Villani, his younger contemporary, presents an entirely different kind of insight into Florentine history.

Born around 1275–80 into a substantial merchant family, sometime around the crucial period which saw the inception of the priorate and the ascendancy of the burgher class, Villani's life, under the influence of his merchant father (Villano di Stoldo), was shaped toward the wealthy interests of the Cerchi, the bitter enemies of the noble Corso Donati and leaders of the White faction.

With the collapse of the Whites and the triumph of the Blacks in 1301, Giovanni prudently spent much of the first decade of the fourteenth century taking care of his father's financial affairs in places like France and Flanders. Upon his return to Florence he became a member of the Black faction, and continued the life which his father's station and success had provided, affiliating himself with the famous banking family, the Peruzzi, and eventually with the Buon-accorsi.

Throughout his life Giovanni fulfilled civic obligations, serving in the highest office of prior in 1316, 1317, and again in 1321. In 1317 he was in charge of the mint, and was responsible for collecting the records up to his time and for providing a register of coins minted in Florence—no small task in the complex systems of money of the time. Toward the end of the next decade he was with the army that was defeated by Castruccio at Altopascio, and was one of the officials appointed to steer Florence through the terrible famine of 1328. In 1330 he superintended the making of the doors by Andrea Pisano for the Baptistry, as well as the raising of the bell tower of the Badia. And in 1331 he was one of the commission charged with the completion of the third wall of the city.

His life in Florence was not one of continuous good fortune, but he had had the satisfaction of a rich participation in its affairs. In 1339, for example, Villani and other rich merchants offered to advance some of the 80,000 florins for the purchase of Lucca, and in 1341, when the acquisition was again being negotiated, this time for 250,000 florins, Giovanni was one of the hostages sent to Mastino della Scala. He was in Florence during the stormy days of the Duke of Athens, and in the great financial crisis of 1345 that bankrupted the Bardi, the Buonaccorsi, the Peruzzi banking families, Villani was also wiped out, spending some time in prison on charges brought against him by one of his creditors. In 1348 he fell victim to the terrible Plague that Boccaccio and he described so vividly.

A mere recitation of the facts of his life enables us to confirm the traits which appear through the long stretches of his *Chronicle:* love for country, zeal in duty, moral rectitude, responsible action. For it is a historical record of the first order, honest, reliable, dispassionate. Although it may lack some of the literary or artistic excitement of Dino's *Chronicle,* it has its own substantial virtues, particularly in those matters which he has personally observed. And from the points of view of statistics, economics, military and social history it provides data which can be garnered from few other sources. His own sources, he tells us, are his personal recollections, his own observations and researches for the period through which he has lived. For the earlier period, like a good medievalist, he borrows heavily from "the most ancient and varied books, chronicles, and writers," the result to be, in his view, a compilation.

Villani's fame rests upon what for him was "modern" history. These newer materials were more within the range of the verifiable, and were gleaned at first hand by active participation in the affairs of state. These materials he appraises with commendable honesty. We can see, from the vantage of later history, that his point of view is that of his class and of his profession, the view of the successful businessman who hates to see the government which insures his success dissipated by the rise to power of the lower castes of Florentine social structure. In matters of faith he remains a man of his time, but in his evaluation of the data of history he is a modern man, offering his own judgments and shaping the materials by intelligent analysis.

Much of what he writes is delivered in a merely factual

way: the recording of earthquake, fire, flood, famine, pestilence, and war in the same dispassionate tone as the vicissitudes of government, the building of bridges, the appointment of officials. There is a consistent moral tone pervading the work which reveals the sober nature of the writer (the calamities that befall man are the justice of God meting out just punishment upon fallen creatures); yet these sections are a valuable source of information about Florence.

We have other grounds on which to be grateful to Giovanni and his ability to transcend political differences. Upon the death of Dante in exile at Ravenna in 1321, he added an encomium to the ninth book of his *Chronicle* (Chapter 136) which is also rich in biographical details. Dante tells us himself that he was charged with barratry; Villani avers that he was driven out simply because of his affiliation with the White faction and "without any other fault." He maintains too that Dante studied at Bologna, and "then at Paris," a datum which has distressed some generations of scholarship, but which, owing to Giovanni's nearness to Dante in time and his general reliability, one is tempted to accept.

Giovanni never tires of statistical data, and this trait has made him the joy and despair of historians. But the data are interesting as well as valuable for the light they throw on such matters as population, schools, hospitals, and the like. Taking general stock of Florence in 1338, he offers the following for posterity: 25,000 men under arms between the ages of fifteen and seventy, among whom are 1,500 nobles and *grandi;* more than 250 knights; total population, on the basis of grain consumed, 90,000 "mouths," including men, women, and children; transients coming and going for various reasons, 1,500, not counting the religious; baptized children, 5,500–6,000, boys being more frequent than girls.

Counting the churches and abbeys, including those of the religious orders, he finds 110, of which 57 are parishes; there are 5 abbeys, 2 priories, 24 monasteries, 10 orders of friars, 30 hospitals with more than 1,000 beds for the poor and infirm. Wool shops number 200 or more, producing between 70,000 and 80,000 "bolts" worth 1,200,000 gold florins, and employing more than 30,000 persons.

Banks numbered 80; judges, 80; notaries, 600; physicians and surgeons, 60; apothecary shops, 100. He adds that it would be impossible to count the number of shops of the various merchandisers and sellers. More than 300 merchants traveled out of Florence on business, as did other workers in wood and stone.

Fire, famine, earthquake, taxes, as well as political events enthralled the mind of our historian throughout his life. Among the calamities which struck Florence in his time were the bouts of pestilence which decimated the population. Both for 1340 and 1348 he remains the clinical observer, and his depiction of the contagion must be ranked with that of Boccaccio. Giovanni Villani's interest in the events of his time transcends such matters as plague, for his account of the pestilence which took his own life is but one chapter in the events of that year. With typical foresight he had left a blank to be filled in to mark the day on which the plague abated, "and the plague lasted till . . . ," a hiatus he never filled in, being overtaken in his early seventies by the disease.

Upon his death his brother Matteo, like him a member of the Buonaccorsi banking firm until its collapse, and a widely informed mind, continued the *Chronicle* which his brother had so faithfully worked on over a period of almost fifty years. The *Chronicle* Matteo carried on up to the year of his own death in the plague of 1363. The eleven books which he supplies have their own merits, but he lacks Giovanni's sharpness of eye and his acute observation.

Filippo, his son, continued the *Chronicle* for the space of a year. His interests were, however, more scholarly than mercantile, and his fame lies elsewhere. He wrote a series of twenty-nine biographical sketches in Latin of the great men of Florence, among them Giotto, Brunetto Latini, Boccaccio, Coluccio Salutati, and Guido Cavalcanti. They are of varying merit. Of considerable interest is his little defense of his father and uncle, whose contribution, as he sees it, was to preserve for posterity much that might have been lost, and thus to provide the stuff out of which more polished historians of the future might recreate the story of the past. His reputation was sufficiently exalted as a scholar to merit his being chosen in 1402, and again in 1404, to lecture on Dante in the chair inaugurated by Boccaccio. With his father and his renowned uncle he completes a triad of witnesses to the shifting currents in the life of his city and that of the illustrious past which they commemorate.

9. Two Bourgeois Writers

CONTEMPORARY WITH BOCCACCIO, a witness like him to the history of Florence, and a bridge between poetry and history is Antonio Pucci (1309–88), bell-ringer, town-crier, minor official, popular poet. From 1333 on he gave free rein to a facile gift of rhyming and poured out verses over the next forty years without ceasing—not merely conventional love sonnets but long romances, moral and didactic poems, historical poems, a long description of the Mercato Vecchio, and a version, in tercets, of Villani's *Chronicle*. Everything in the common life of Florence was a subject for his pen, and besides poems on the flood of 1333, the famine of 1346, and the war with Pisa in 1362–64, he could submit to rhyme a list of the illustrious families of Florence.

Even his little garden with its figs and jessamine and its little corner of oaks he put into terza rima, as Sacchetti tells us, "like the poem of Dante." Obviously he found his materials everywhere, and the question of poetical values aside, his voracious appetite for the sights and sounds, occurrences and events of his own life and that around him has made him for posterity a valuable witness of his age. Ever interesting in these terms, he gives evidence of feelings and responses always on the surface of life, of writing quickly and without deep thought. He is, furthermore, lavish with moral comment and didactic utterance which reflect the common attitudes of his time.

177

We may understand the limitations of Antonio Pucci's work if we recognize it for what it is—popular poetry in which common sense takes the place of deep thought, and simplicity of sentiment takes the place of deep emotion. It does not set up in our inward being those fugitive stirrings of which Wordsworth spoke so knowingly, nor does it aim at anything greater than a merely adequate diction. The rhythms, too, are vocal rhythms, meant for expressive recitation. Pucci's poems are mainly addressed to listeners and in all probability were actually recited by the poet himself. We must recognize, however, that popular poetry often strives toward the highest kinds and occasionally touches more than the immediate sentiment—in short, becomes poetry.

Occasionally a strain of bitterness enters the poems, particularly those on poverty or the corruption of magistrates. A long description of the encroachment of old age, a topic which we meet many times in medieval literature, takes us through the horrors one by one, not only the physical defects of age but the moral ones as well: the easy rages, the boasting, the avarice, the lies. The tradition we recognize as one that goes back to Juvenal and Maximian, and we meet it on English soil in Chaucer's Reeve.

In a long poem, something between a satire and a moral treatise, Pucci enumerates his pet peeves: haughty, pompous, or witty priests; sleepers in church; loud prayers; smilers at funerals; scorn of the gentleman; gossiping; the breaking of friendship over trifles; much ado about nothing; garrulity and boasting; those who dress beyond their means; denigrators; those who come to dine or drink uninvited; those who sit down to dine without washing their hands; those who sit at table with legs crossed, or stretched under so far as to annoy others; persons who crack nuts with their teeth; noisy eaters; and so on in a sequence of items rich in suggestions of the time. In the more personal utterances they are surprisingly vivid and revelatory of life itself, as when he complains of those who put their hands in their purses as if to pay—but don't, or of those who chastise their family before strangers, or of those who blow on their food to cool it. His ninety-six complaints lack a really incisive or corrosive bitterness, and fall rather into the category of an assumed pose of crotchetiness. The title "Noie" indicates the subject: peeves or annoyances.

The only time Pucci approaches excitement is in his description of the Mercato Vecchio, its streets, its corner churches, its doctors and apothecaries, its various merchants and their shops, the foodstuffs, fruits and meats, eggs and chickens, the hectic press of whores and pimps, gamblers, cheats, and beggars—all creating such an atmosphere of excitement as to lead the poet to breathless exaggeration. The poem is replete with little vignettes of the commoner life of Florence, often neglected in historical accounts, offering insights into the humbler classes and their diversions.

This is the real Pucci and his more characteristic voice. If the recitation of foodstuffs offered for sale on the various holidays seems excessive, or the account of knife-murders a trifle glib, it is nonetheless vivacious, enthusiastic, and swift; it is, furthermore, extremely personal, a kind of love letter to Florence, expressing Pucci's gratitude at a life so rich and diversified as to become the subject of his song.

The last substantial voice of the century is that of Franco Sacchetti (1330?–1400?), a somewhat sad witness to the end of a great age of poetry. The writer of several hundred poems, a collection of commentaries on Biblical texts, some letters, and a lively body of tales from his last years, he is in many ways a compendium of ideas and forms which the lamented past had developed and outworn. Although he is in many of his poems a somewhat jejune rhymer, he is in the madrigals, the ballate, and the *caccie,* some of which he or his friend Francesco degli Organi set to music, lively and pleasing; the Biblical texts on which he meditates are sanely treated, with a great deal of art and wisdom; and the tales which he collects in the last years of his life are as lively and authentic a depiction of the era through which he lived as we find anywhere in the century.

Sacchetti was himself of a noble family which Dante recalls in the *Paradiso* as among the most ancient of the city. Trained for the merchant's life, he wrote verses from his early years and engaged in exchanges of poems with many of the poets of his age. Like many another of the noble descendants he fulfilled civic responsibilities, eventually giving up the world of business for that of politics, serving in a variety of capacities over the course of his adult years.

Much of his life was plagued by misfortunes: he outlived two of his three wives, endured a number of ailments and injuries, suffered financial setbacks, and toward the end of his life was made virtually bankrupt by damage to his property by a company of soldiers of fortune. But through it all he remained a staunch, moral man, with powers of keen observation and considerable wit. His poems, meditations, and tales are touched by a persistently moral point of view which sometimes overrides the more cynical implications of the realism they contain; and his knowledge of human psychology puts him almost in a class with Boccaccio.

He reveals himself in his personal letters as a critic of

his time, charging the people with naïveté in faith as they dash from shrine to shrine, loading church walls with so many pictures that if the walls were not bolstered, the roof would cave in; lambasting the clergy for their cupidity; and in general attacking all forms of sham and hypocrisy. And when his friends see his woes as the result of his speaking out against war, he answers shrewdly that if this is so he is happy then to have suffered, and sorry for those who have not.

His meditations on Scripture are mainly ethical rather than theological, bordering upon social commentary. He does not hesitate to speak out, as in his personal letters, against forms of hypocrisy among laity as well as clergy, against various forms of injustice, ignorance, or indifference to the common good. Sometimes his reasoning is daring, as when he asks, on the subject of love, "Does God want me to love the Devil?" and answers, "Yes, inasmuch as he is a creature of God." More often he has the air of a man asking questions fearlessly of his faith, deliberating matters not immediately within the scope of religion. The consistency of his thinking is remarkable in that the sermons, written in 1378 and after, contain views to which he clings in his later tales and poems.

He reverts to Dante on the salvation of heathens who know not baptism, on the ineffableness of God's justice; and where he does not actually quote his great predecessor, his views arise out of the same intellectual tradition, and the points made are arrived at by dialectical method. Like Dante too, he is a passionate proponent of peace and a blistering commentator upon the degeneracy of the age. He is still medieval in his ascription of power over men's bodies to the planets, but like the intellectuals of his time he believed wholeheartedly in man's essential freedom. In his discussions of the various sins, for example on the insatiable appetite of the miser, on envy, or on lust, he sees eye to eye with St. Augustine and places the responsibility upon the individual.

His poems, too, reveal a sane response to the disturbances of his age. Seeing the end of civil strife in 1378 after the riots of the Ciompi, he wrote to the new government, pleading for a return to prudent government committed to protecting the innocent and restoring temperate action to the affairs of the state. It is a conventional utterance, but one which places Florentine politics within the sane perspectives of an ancient tradition, and gives us a clue of Sacchetti's own hopes for a middle path between the oligarchic control of the nobles and the chaotic pressures of the masses. And toward the end of his life, twelve sonnets on peace are a heartfelt plea for a time when suspicion and bloodshed will be over and old customs may be restored.

Two *canzoni* on the deaths of Petrarch and of Boccaccio are famous for Sacchetti's recognition of the passing of a great era in Italian literary history. Heaven rejoices while earth weeps, now that Petrarch is dead. And when Boccaccio has died, he laments that poetry has now disappeared and that the mansions of Parnassus are empty. Death has taken one by one the intellectuals of the age. In the general dearth which has overcome Florence, where shall we find someone to lecture on Dante?

> *The summoning horns have blown*
> *On every side.*
> *Summer has passed and gone.*
> *When it will return I cannot say,*
> *But not soon . . . .*

In these lines Sacchetti gives us a sad glimpse of the age.

A happier group of poems are the madrigals, the ballate. Graceful and vivacious, some of them elegant in a way that looks forward to the Renascence, they bear the superscript *"Francus dedit sonum,"* or the names of Lorenzo da Firenze or Niccolò, the names of those who set the pieces to music. To these we may add a small number of *caccie,* poems of an extremely irregular meter moving rapidly through a scene presented almost entirely in breathless dialogue. The most popular deals with a group of girls who see a snake while gathering flowers and flee in a sudden shower, leaving their flowers behind, a poem of real charm, in keeping with a pastoral mood in which Sacchetti often writes with astonishing vigor, grace, and charm. In all probability, the musical forms in which he wrote are ultimately French in origin, musical theory and practice having received new impetus from the work of Philippe de Vitry and Guillaume de Machaut. The new music was characterized by complexity in the musical line, greater demand upon the voice, dissonances, and an air of improvisation. Suited to poems, this music becomes a graceful adjunct to fourteenth-century life.

Nonetheless, Sacchetti's reputation in posterity rests not on his poems, nor on his letters and sermons or meditations, but upon the collection of stories called *The Three Hundred Tales.* The collection actually contains 223 tales (of these 8 are fragments), the remainder having been lost in the passage of time. They were the fruit of Franco's last years, while he was acting as podesta in a variety of northern cities, the distillation of long experience in the world.

The inevitable comparison that is raised is that of Sacchetti with Boccaccio. It is true that almost everything in the way of intellectual range, of realistic tone, is present in

Boccaccio, that he is incomparably the greater literary artist. But this is precisely their difference. Boccaccio had literary intentions in the handling of prose, in the shaping of narrative, in the structuring of the whole *Decameron*. Sacchetti did not. He is modest about his abilities and modest about his intentions. More than anything else he is writing a book of memoirs—things he saw, heard, did. He seems to have no design, like that of Boccaccio (or that of Giovanni Fiorentino and Giovanni Sercambi), other than the casual grouping of tales about certain persons or subjects. His purpose, however unambitious, includes moral reflection imposed upon the tales. This sententiousness we note in Sacchetti from his early maturity, after the crises of the late seventies and early eighties, as a permanent part of his plain art.

The scenes of his tales are restricted to Tuscany and Romagna, with Florence figuring in a great number of them, and the persons who are featured in the tales are of course familiar to the student of Italian history: artists, great lords, poets, soldiers of fortune, jesters, popes, kings, judges, priors, governors, and minor functionaries; and everywhere, as in Antonio Pucci, the common people, the shopkeepers, tradesmen, market-women, soldiers, beggars, in the places the traveler today can re-people in his imagination—the Mercato Vecchio, the Piazza della Signoria, the streets and bridges of the old city.

His example is that of Boccaccio, whose *Decameron* had achieved such popularity as to be translated into French and English, but the realistic vision of life presented in the tales is his own. There is no room here for the purely tragic view—Sacchetti's genius does not soar. The anecdotal nature of the tales precludes anything but the most rapid sketching in of the characters of his agents, with their psychology quickly stated, so that they may serve the needs of the plot.

The tales offer the fulfillment of his talent for the spoken word, the ironical situation, the grotesqueric of the human situation. He cannot resist adding to these the preachments of a man who had lived long and observed much. He has seen men driven by power, he has observed the boaster, the miser, the cheat, the hypocrite and the charlatan, the corrupted and the corrupting. All of these he reviews within the scope of a satirical and moral vision.

Some of the stories, as in all large collections of tales, are banal, trivial, and even pointless. Some of them are inflated by a self-conscious, gratuitous commentary from the author; about some of them is a mediocrity and a want of grace; but they are, in their anecdotal sections, straightforward, vivid, rapid in execution; the portraits of many of the agents are done with slashing and unsparing honesty, as though the passage of the years had sharpened Sacchetti's eye to see to the very bones and marrow, to the skull beneath the flesh. They are, in short, the tales of an old man, whom only good nature saves from the entirely bitter and choleric, and in whom profound sadness at the decline of the age has been partly salvaged by religious resignation.

Sacchetti has been called the last of the writers of the *trecento,* and perhaps there is something significant in the fact that his death occurs at the very end of the century. Much of what he wrote was a memorial to a great past which to his great sorrow could never return. One feels a fatigue in Sacchetti; he saw in his personal plight, at the end of his days, the decline of the world. He thought that the divine trumpet would sound, calling vengeance upon the sins

185

of the world, assigning men to a place from which there is no return. But a human trumpet had sounded; new life came with the new century, and a whole generation of men with new ideas were ready to take their place in the march of history. Sacchetti's middling views unfortunately kept him apart from the new world of learning which was being born as he was dying. By the time of his death the new age had stirred, had risen, and was ready. Whether for better or worse, the historians of art, of literature, of culture, of politics must each in their turn say.

Selected Bibliography

1. Politics and History

Baron, Hans. *The Crisis of the Early Italian Renaissance.* 2 vols. Princeton University Press, 1955.

——. *Humanistic and Political Literature in Florence and Venice.* Harvard University Press, 1955.

Bowsky, William M. *Henry VII in Italy; The Conflict of Empire and City-State, 1310–1313.* University of Nebraska Press, 1960.

Brucker, Gene A. *Florentine Politics and Society, 1343–1378.* Princeton University Press, 1962.

Compagni, Dino. *The Chronicle.* Trans. by Else C. M. Benecke and A. G. Ferrers Howell. Temple Classics. London, 1906.

Machiavelli, Niccolò. *Florentine History.* Trans. by W. K. Marriott. Everyman's Library. London, 1922.

Pucci, E. *A Short History of Florence from Its Origins to Italian Unity.* Trans. by C. Danyell Tassinari. Florence, 1939.

Schevill, Ferdinand. *History of Florence from the Founding of the City through the Renaissance.* New York, 1936.

Villani, Giovanni. *Selections from the First Nine Books of the Chroniche fiorentine of Giovanni Villani.* Trans. by Rose E. Selfe; ed. by P. H. Wicksteed. Westminster, 1896.

Villani, Pasquale. *The First Two Centuries of Florentine*

History: The Republic and Parties at the Time of Dante. Trans. by Linda Villari. New York, 1894–95.

2. Society and Culture

Biagi, Guido. *Men and Manners of Old Florence; Essays on Florentine Life and Manners.* Chicago, 1909.

Burckhardt, Jacob C. *The Civilization of the Renaissance in Italy, an Essay.* Trans. by S. G. C. Middlemore. Oxford University Press, 1944.

Edler, Florence. *Glossary of Mediaeval Terms of Business.* Mediaeval Academy of America. Cambridge, Mass., 1934.

Heywood, William. *Palio and Ponte; An Account of the Sports of Central Italy from the Age of Dante to the XXth Century.* London, 1904.

Niccolini di Camugliano, Ginevra. *The Chronicles of a Florentine Family, 1200–1470.* London, 1933.

Origo, Iris. *The Merchant of Prato, Francesco di Marco Datini.* London, 1957.

————. *The World of San Bernardino.* London, 1962.

Robb, Nesca A. *Platonism of the Italian Renaissance.* London, 1935.

Sellery, George Clarke. *The Renaissance, Its Nature and Origins.* University of Wisconsin Press, 1950.

Staley, Edgcumbe. *The Guilds of Florence.* London, 1906.

Symonds, John A. *The Renaissance in Italy.* 7 vols. New York, 1888. [The volumes *The Revival of Learning* and *The Fine Arts* are of special interest.]

3. Painting, Sculpture, and Architecture

Antal, Frederick. *Florentine Painting and Its Social Background.* London, 1947.

Bargellini, Piero. *Florence, An Appreciation of Her Beauty.* Florence, 1956.

Brown, James Wood. *The Builders of Florence.* London, 1907.

Crichton, George H. *Nicola Pisano and the Revival of Sculpture in Italy.* Cambridge, Eng., 1938.

————. *Romanesque Sculpture in Italy.* London, 1954.

Decker, Heinrich. *Romanesque Art in Italy.* Trans. from the German by James Cleugh. New York, 1959.

Gardner, Edmund G. *Florence and Its Story.* Medieval Town Series. London (Revised), 1953.

Hauser, Arnold. *The Social History of Art.* 2 vols. London, 1951.

Krey, August Charles. *A City That Art Built.* University of Minnesota Press, 1936.

Meiss, Millard. *Painting in Florence and Siena after the Black Death.* Princeton University Press, 1951.

Pope-Hennesey, John. *Italian Gothic Sculpture.* Phaidon Publishers, Inc., New York, 1955.

Van Marle, Raimond. *The Development of the Italian Schools of Painting.* 19 vols. The Hague, 1923–38.

Vasari, Giorgio. *The Lives of the Painters, Sculptors, and Architects.* Trans. by A. B. Hinds. 4 vols. Everyman's Library. New York, 1927.

Venturi, Adolfo. *A Short History of Italian Art.* New York, 1926.

4. Literature and Biography

Barbi, Michele. *The Life of Dante.* Trans. by Paul G. Ruggiers. University of California Press. 1954.

Boase, T. S. R. *Boniface VIII.* Makers of the Middle Ages. London, 1933.

Boccaccio, Giovanni. *The Decameron of Giovanni Boccac-*

189

cio. Newly trans. by Frances Winwar, with an Introduction by Burton Rascoe. New York, 1930.

————. *The Earliest Lives of Dante*. Trans. from the Italian of Boccaccio and Lionardo Bruni Aretino by James Robinson Smith. New York, 1901.

Chubb, Thomas C. *The Life of Giovanni Boccaccio*. New York, 1930.

Hall, Robert A., Jr. *A Short History of Italian Literature*. Ithaca, N. Y., 1949.

MacManus, Francis. *Boccaccio*. Writers of the World. London, 1947.

Osgood, Charles G. *Boccaccio on Poetry*. Princeton University Press, 1930.

Sacchetti, Franco. *Tales from Sacchetti*. Trans. from the Italian by Mary G. Steegman, with an Introduction by Dr. Guido Biagi. London, 1908.

Salutati, Coluccio. "De Tyranno" and "Letters in Defence of Liberal Studies," in *Humanism and Tyranny; Studies in the Italian Trecento,* by Ephraim Emerton. Harvard University Press, 1925.

Sanctis, Francesco de. *A History of Italian Literature*. 2 vols. Trans. by Linda Redfern. New York, 1931.

Tatham, Edward H. R. *Francesco Petrarca, the First Modern Man of Letters; His Life and Correspondence*. 2 vols. London, 1926.

Whitfield, J. H. *Petrarch, Man of the Renaissance*. London, 1947.

Wilkins, Ernest Hatch. *A History of Italian Literature*. Harvard University Press, 1954.

————. *Life of Petrarch*. University of Chicago Press, 1961.

————. *Petrarch at Vaucluse*. University of Chicago Press, 1958.

Index

191

Index